Rugby songs are sung wherever Rugby
is played, and in a lot of other places
besides. This unique and
comprehensive collection of more
than 140 songs ranges from such all-
time favourites as 'Eskimo Nell'
and 'The Good Ship Venus' to
lesser known but equally worthy gems
gathered from every corner of the
world

Why Was He Born So Beautiful

and Other Rugby Songs

With a Preface by Michael Green

* SPHERE HUMOUR CLASSICS *

SPHERE BOOKS LIMITED
London and Sydney

First published in Great Britain by
Sphere Books Ltd 1967
30–32 Gray's Inn Road, London WC1X 8JL
This collection copyright © Harry Morgan 1967
Preface copyright © Michael Green 1967
Reprinted 1973, 1976, 1978 (twice), 1979,
1980, 1981, 1982, 1984, 1985

TRADE
MARK

Set in Linotype Baskerville

Printed and bound in Great Britain by
Collins, Glasgow

Editorial Note: For more specialised insights into the social psychology of these songs, and to the fans who evidently take pleasure from singing them, a recent article by the eminent psychiatrist Dr. Stafford Clark is recommended.

The Publishers acknowledge that some of the songs in this volume may bear a relationship, however denatured, to other poems or hymns actually written by poets intent on purposes other than conviviality. There may even be some of those authors who, not being rugby fans, consider that the present version of their work deserves, if not suppression, some acknowledgement to its original creator. In the absence of such credit, which might in too many cases have justifiably annoyed the originator from whose work the lyric here included was derived, the Publishers apologise to the poets. If any of you who can prove ownership wish credit in the form of cash and are prepared to come forward, at whatever risk to reputation or good name, the Publishers are prepared to negotiate a reasonable settlement – quietly, and out of court.

Contents

Preface

By Michael Green
(Author of *The Art of Coarse Rugby*)

It has often been said that what happens after a game of rugby is more important than what happens on the field and the sing-song is one of the chief post-match activities. Perhaps it is rather stretching it to use the word "sing". The noise which comes out of a rugby clubhouse on Saturday night has little in common with the world of Maria Callas and Benjamin Britten, although the dissonant half-tones, like an elderly bagpipe exploding, which mark attempts at harmony, might gladden the heart of a Kurdistan shepherd.

Yet the rugby song does have a crude sort of folk-culture all of its own. At its worst it is simply a bawdy chorus, a Chaucerian obsession with the basic functions of the human body being the essential linking theme of all good rugby songs. At its best it may tell a moving story or make a pertinent social comment. Keir Hardie himself could not have resisted the Socialist appeal of "They're Digging up Father's Grave to Build a Sewer", the story or an honest British workman who was exhumed for the building of a sewer up to "some dirty posh's residence" and who retaliated by haunting the aristocrats' lavatory seat. And his heart would be hard indeed who was not moved by the tragedy of Morphine Bill and Cocaine Sue who after killing themselves with drugs ("Honey have a sniff have a sniff on me") were buried side by side.

Some rugby songs tell a narrative story of heroic proportions in *recitative*, such as the famous "Eskimo Nell" or the witty story of the incredible "Wild West Show", from which the word Oozelum Bird has passed into the language as a symbol of futility. Others, like "Oh, You Zulu Warriors" depend for their appeal on violent physical actions by the participants, such as pouring beer over the singer. A large section are derived from hymn tunes, and while the version of "Hark my soul, it is the Lord" would scarcely be accepted by ecclesiastical authorities, it has a grim attraction of its own.

Truly there is something for everybody, providing they can drink enough beer to dull their finer senses. Now, for the first time, some of these historic ditties are gathered together in one volume which will form a treasure trove for the psychologist. This book fills a gap in English Literature (somewhere between Smollett and Henry Miller, I think). I commend it to all rugby players who can read, while even front-row forwards will enjoy having it spelled out for them.

DID YOU EVER SEE

Oh, I got an Aunty Sissy,
And she's only got one titty,
But it's very long and pointed
And the nipple's double jointed.

Chorus: Did you ever see,
Did you ever see,
Did you ever see,
Such a funny thing before.

I've got a cousin Daniel,
And he's got a cocker spaniel,
If you tickled 'im in the middle
He would lift his leg and piddle.

Oh, I've got a cousin Rupert,
He plays outside half for Newport.
They think so much about him
That they always play without him.

Oh, I've got a cousin Anna,
And she's got a grand piana,
And she ram aram arama,
Till the neighbours say "God Damn Her."

LULU

Some girls work in factories,
some girls work in stores,
But my girl works in a knockin' shop
with forty other whores.

Chorus: Oh bang away Lulu, bang away Lulu
  Bang away good and strong,
  Whata we to do for a good blow through,
  When Lulu's dead and gone?

Lulu had a baby, it was an awful shock
She couldn't call it Lulu 'cos
the bastard had a ****.

I took her to the pictures,
we sat down in the stalls,
And every time the lights went out
she grabbed me by the *****.

She and I went fishing in a dainty punt
And every time I hooked a sprat
she stuffed it up her ****.

I wish I was a silver ring
upon my Lulu's hand
And every time she scratched her ****
I'd see the promised land.

I wish I was a chamber pot under Lulu's bed,
And every time she took a piss
I'd see her maidenhead.

DARLING GRACE

Oh darling Grace
I love your face,
I love you in your nightie,
When the moonlight flits
Across your tits
Oh Jesus Christ Almighty.

LIL

Although a lady of ill-repute
Lilian Barker was a beaut,
And it was really deemed an honour
To be allowed to climb upon her.

Her lovely face was smooth and fair,
And golden was her flowing hair,
Yet pot and hash and cruel cocaine
Had ravaged heart and soul and brain.

Lil could take with sly content
A trooper of his regiment,
Hyperbole it sometimes seems,
Is not confined to wishful dreams.

But soon she had to see a doctor
To find out what disease had pocked her.
The diagnosis short and clear
Revealed a dose of gonorrhoea.

As Lilian lay in her disgrace,
She felt the devil kiss her face,
She said, "Now mate I'm always willing
But first let's see your silver shilling."

Three old whores from Winnipeg
Were drinking cherry wine,
Says one of them to the other two,
"Yours is smaller than mine."

Chorus: So take up the sheets me hearties,
Water the decks with brine;
Bend to the oars, you lousy whores,
None is bigger than mine.

"You're a liar", says the second old whore,
"Mine's as big as the sea,
The battle ships sail in and out
And never a bother to me."

"You're a liar", says the third old whore,
"Mine's as big as the moon,
The battle ships sail in
on the first of the year,
They never come out till June."

"You're a liar", says the first again,
Mine's as big as the air,
The battle ships sail in and out,
They never tickle a hair."

"You're a liar", says the second again,
"Mine is bigger than all,
For many the ships that sail right in,
And they never come out at all."

YOUNG ROGER OF KILDARE

Oh, mother, mother, dear
May I go to the fair
May I go with young Roger
Young Roger of Kildare
For I know he's kind and gentle
And will love me for my sake
And I know he will not harm me
Coming home from the wake.

Oh, daughter, daughter, dear
You may go to the fair
You may go with young Roger
Young Roger of Kildare
For I know he's kind and gentle
And will love you for your sake
But keep your legs close together
Coming home from the wake.

So she went to the fair
So she went to the fair
She went with young Roger
Young Roger of Kildare
So he stuffed her up with ice-cream
And he stuffed her up with cake
And he stuffed it right up her
Coming home from the wake.

THE TRAVELLER

I came home on Saturday night
as drunk as I could be,
And there was a hat upon the rack
where my hat ought to be,
So I said to my wife, the curse of my life,
"Explain this thing to me,
Whose is that hat upon the rack
where my hat ought to be?"

  "Oh, you're drunk, you fool,
    You daft old fool,
      As drunk as a **** can be
      That's not a hat upon the rack
      But a chamberpot you see."
Well, I've travelled this wide world over,
ten thousand miles or more,
But a jerry with a hatband on
I never saw before.

I came home on Saturday night
as drunk as I could be,
And there was a horse in the stable
where my horse ought to be,
So I said to my wife, the curse of my life,
"Explain this thing to me,
Whose is this horse in the stable
where my horse ought to be?"

  "Oh, you're drunk, you fool,
    You daft old fool,
      As drunk as a **** can be,
      That's not a horse in the stable
      But a milch cow you can see."

Well, I've travelled this wide world over,
ten thousand miles or more,
But a milch cow with a saddle on
I never saw before.

I came home on Saturday night
as drunk as I could be,
And there were some breeks beside the bed
where my breeks ought to be,
So I said to my wife, the curse of my life,
"Explain this thing to me,
Whose are those breeks a-lying
where my breeks ought to be?"
   "Oh, you're drunk, you fool,
    You daft old fool,
    As drunk as a **** can be,
     Those aren't a pair of breeches
     But a polishing cloth you see."
Well, I've travelled this wide world over,
a thousand miles or more,
But a polishing cloth with buttons on
I never saw before.

I came home on Saturday night as
drunk as I could be,
And there was a head on the pillow
where my head ought to be,
So I said to my wife, the curse of my life,
"Explain this thing to me,
Whose is this head a-lying there
where my head ought to be?"

"Oh, you're drunk, you fool,
    You daft old fool,
    As drunk as a **** can be,
    That's not a head on the pillow,
    But a mushmelon you see."
Well, I've travelled this wide world over,
ten thousand miles or more,
But a mushmelon with a moustache
I never saw before.

I came home on Saturday night
as drunk as I could be
And there was a **** inside my bed
where my **** ought to be,
So I said to my wife, the curse of my life,
"Explain this thing to me,
Whose is this **** a-standing here
where my **** ought to be?"
    "Oh, you're drunk, you fool,
    You daft old fool,
    As drunk as a **** can be,
    That's not a **** a-standing there,
    But a carrot that you see."
Well, I've travelled this wide world over,
ten thousand miles or more,
But a carrot with ******** on
I never saw before.

I came home on Saturday night
as drunk as I could be,

There was a stain on the counterpane,
and it didn't come from me,
So I said to my wife, the curse of my life,
"Explain this thing to me,
What's this stain on the counterpane
which doesn't come from me?"
  "Oh, you're drunk, you fool,
    You daft old fool,
    As drunk as a **** can be,
    That's not a stain on the counterpane
    But some baby's milk you see."

Well, I've travelled this wide world over,
ten thousand miles or more,
But baby's milk that smelt like cum
I've never smelt before.

CAN YOU WALK A LITTLE WAY
WITH IT IN?

Can you walk a little way with it in,
with it in,
Can you walk a little way with it in,
with it in
She answered with a smile
I can walk a ******* mile
With it in
With it in
With it in.

The working class
Can kiss my ****,
I've got the foreman's job at last.
I'm out of work,
And on the dole
You can stuff the red flag
Up your hole.

'Twas on Gibraltar's rock, so fair,
I saw a maiden lying there
And as she lay in sweet repose,
A puff of wind blew up her clothes,
A sailor who was passing by
Tipped his hat and winked his eye.
And then he saw to his despair
She had the red flag flying there.

NELLIE 'AWKINS

I first met Nellie 'Awkins
down the Old Kent Road.
Her drawers were hanging down,
'Cos she'd been with Charlie Brown,
I pressed a filthy tanner
in her filthy bleeding hand.
'Cos she was a low down whore.

She wore no blouses
And I wore no trousers,
And she wore no underclothes,
And when she caressed me
She damn near undressed me
It's a thrill that no one knows.
I went to the doctor,
He said, "Where did you block 'er?"
I said, "Down where the green grass grows."
He said, quick as a twinkle,
The pimple on your winkle
Will be bigger than a red, red rose."

THE MOLE CATCHER

In Manchester city
by the sign of The Plough
There lived a mole catcher,
I can't tell you how,

Chorus:
With his la ti lie diddle,
and his la ti lie day.

He'd go out mole catching
from morning till night,
And a young fellow would come
for to visit his wife.

Now the mole catcher got jealous
of all the same thing,
And he hid under the wash house
to see what did come in.

Now this young fellow
comes climbing over the stile,
And the mole catcher's watching
with a crafty smile.

He knocks at the door and this he does say,
"Where is your husband,
good woman, I pray?"

"He's gone out mole catching,
you have nothing to fear."
Little did she know
the old bastard was near.

They went up the stairs
and she gives him the sign,
But the filthy old fellow did creep up behind.

Now just as the young fellow
reached the height of his frolics,
The mole catcher grabs him quite fast
by the ********.

The trap it squeezed tighter,
the mole catcher did smile,
"Here's the best mole
we've caught in a while."

"I'll make you pay well
for ploughing me ground
This little prank will cost you
all of ten pound."

"Oh," says the young fellow,
"Christ gov, I don't mind,
For it only works out at tuppence a grind."

So come all you young fellows
and mind what you're at,
Don't ever get yours caught
in a mole catcher's trap.

THE RING DANG DOO

I got a gal in New Orleans,
She's young, just sweet sixteen,
She's young, and pretty too,
And she's got what they call
The Ring Dang Doo.

Chorus : Now the Ring Dang Doo
        Pray, what is that?
        So soft and round like a pussy cat,
        So soft and round and split in two,
        That's what they call the Ring
           Dang Doo.

She took me down into her cellar,
She said I was a very fine feller,
She fed me with wine,
And whiskey too,
And she let me play
with her Ring Dang Doo.

She took me up into her bed,
Placed a pillow beneath my head,
Took out my **** a doodle—doo,
And stuck it in her Ring Dang Doo.

Now her mother said, "You goddam fool,
You have broken the golden rule,
So pack your bags and your suitcase too,
And go to hell with your Ring Dang Doo."

Now she went to town to become a whore,
She placed a sign upon her door,
"Two dollars down, the rest I'll do,
To take a crack at my Ring Dang Doo."

They came by fours, they came by twos,
First came the Japs, then came the Jews,
Then came the sailors, the Marines too,
Till they damn near ruined
her Ring Dang Doo.

The army came and the army went,
The price went down to fifty cents,
They got the clap and the scabadoo,
When they all took a crack at
her Ring Dang Doo.

And now she's dead and buried deep,
Her body lies on Chestnut Street,
Her tits hang on the city wall
And her pussy floats in alcohol.

RING THE BELL, VERGER

Down in the belfry chauffeur lies,
Vicar's wife between his thighs,
Voice from pulpit from afar,
"Stop ******* wife
and start ******* car."

Chorus: Ring the bell, verger,
           ring the bell, ring,
           Perhaps the congregation
           will condescend to sing.
           Perhaps the village organist,
           sitting on his stool,
           Will play upon his organ,
           and not upon his ****.

Verger in the belfry stood,
Grasped in his hand, his mighty pud.
From afar the vicar yells,
"Stop pulling pud,
and pull ******* bells."

Ocean liner six days late,
Stoker stoking stoker's mate,
Voice from Captain o'er the wire,
"Stop poking mate, start poking fire."

*In the Street of a Thousand ****holes*
Neath the sign of the swinging tit,
There lived a Chinese maiden
*By the name of U-Flung-****.*

*Chorus: Her greasy ****
         Was forever hot
         U-Flung-****,
         her name, her name,
         U-Flung-**** her name.*

She sat beneath the joss sticks
With a smile of celestial bliss,
Her breath like scented lotus,
Her eyes like pools of piss.

She thought of her lover, the bastard,
She thought of her pox-ridden beaux,
She thought of the scores she's had
on the floors,
When up walked Wun-Hung-Low.

*"Oh come to me, you bag of ****."*
He cried with tits in hand,
"My love for you will last for hours
Like ice upon the desert sand."

She raised herself on her starboard tit,
*And gave her **** a tweak,*
With smiles in her eyes she looked at him
*And said: "Go **** a Peke."*

He clutched his **** with calloused hand
And beat it on the walls,
Removed his hat and trampled that
Then danced upon his ****.

At length with anger screaming out
He pissed himself with spleen
He went and **** and stamped in it,
His scrotum turned quite green.

His anger quickly mastered him,
He fell with fury black,
She stood on him and bared her ****
And pissed on the bugger's back.

The Chinese maiden now is gone.
No longer does she sit
In the Street of a Thousand ****holes
By the sign of the swinging tit.

A is for ****holes all covered in hair,
Chorus: Heigh Ho said Rolly.
B is the Bugger that wishes he were there,
Chorus: With a rolly polly,
  up 'em and stuff 'em,
  Heigh Ho said Anthony Rolly.

C is for **** all dripping with piss
D is the Drunkard who gave it a kiss.

E is for Eunuch with only one ball.
F is for ****** with no balls at all.

G is for Gonorrhoea, Goitre and Gout,
H is for Harlot that spread it about.

I is Injection for clap, pox and itch.
J is for Jerk of a dog on a bitch.

K is for King who thought ******* a bore,
L is for Lesbian who came back for more.

M is for Maidenhead tattered and torn.
N is for Noble who died with a horn.

O is for Orifice gently revealed.
P is for ***** all Pranged up and Peeled.

Q is the Quaker who **** in his hat,
R is the Roger who rogered the cat.

S is the **** pot all full to the brim.
T is the turds that are floating within.

31

U is the Usher who taught us at school.
V is the Virgin that played with his ****.

W is the Whore
who thought ******* a farce.
X, Y and Z you can stuff up your ****.

ALL THE NICE GIRLS LOVE A CANDLE

All the nice girls love a candle,
All the nice girls love a wick,
For there's something about a candle
Which reminds them of a *****.
Nice and greasy, slips in easy,
It's a girly's pride and joy,
It's been up our Lady Jane
And it's going up again,
Ship ahoy, ship ahoy.

THERE WAS A PRIEST, THE DIRTY BEAST

There was a priest, the dirty beast,
Whose name was Alexander.
His mighty ***** was inches thick
He called it Salamander.

One night he slept with the Gypsy Queen,
Whose face was black as charcoal,
But in the dark he missed his mark,
And sparks came out her ****hole.

A brat was born one rainy morn,
With a face as black as charcoal,
It had a ***** ten inches thick
But it didn't have an ****hole.

THE BALL OF KERRYMUIR

Oh the Ball, the Ball of Kerrymuir,
Where your wife and my wife,
Were a-doing on the floor.

Chorus : Balls to your partner,
*   ***** against the wall,*
*   If you never get ******,*
*   on a Saturday night*
*   You'll never be ****** at all.*

Four and twenty virgins
Came down from Inverness,
And when the ball was over
There were four and twenty less.

Four and twenty prostitutes
Came up from Glockamore
And when the ball was over
They were all of them double bore.

The village plumber he was there
He felt an awful fool
He'd come eleven leagues or more
And forgot to bring his tool.

*There was ******* in the hallways*
*And ******* in the ricks,*
You couldn't hear the music
*For the swishing of the ******.*

*There was ******* in the kitchen,*
*And ******* in the halls,*
You couldn't hear the music for
*The clanging of the *****.*

*There was ******* in the ante-room,*
*And ******* on the stairs,*
You couldn't see the carpet
*For the ***** and curly hairs.*

Sandy McPherson he came along,
It was a bloody shame,
*He ****** a lassie forty times*
And wouldna take her haim.

The parson's daughter she was there,
The cunning little runt,
*With poison ivy up her ****
*And thistle up her ****.*

The Vicar's wife, well she was there,
A-sitting by the fire
Knitting rubber Johnnies
Out of india rubber tyre.

The village idiot he was there,
Sitting on a pole,
He pulled his foreskin over his head
And whistled through the hole.

Mrs O'Maley she was there
She had the crowd in fits

A-jumping off the mantelpiece
And bouncing off her tits.

The bride was in the kitchen
Explaining to the groom
That the vagina not the rectum
Is the entrance to the womb.

The village magician he was there,
Up to his favourite trick,
Pulling his ****hole over his head
And standing on his *****.

The village smithy he was there,
Sitting by the fire,
Doing abortions by the score
With a piece of red hot wire.

The blacksmith's brother he was there,
A mighty man was he,
He lined them up against the wall
And ****** them three by three.

Now farmer Giles he was there,
His sickle in his hand
And every time he swung around
He circumcised the band.

The Vicar's wife she was there,
Back against the wall,
"Put your money on the table, boys,
I'm fit to do ye all."

The Vicar and his wife
Were having lots of fun,
The parson had his finger
Up another lady's bum.

There was ******* on the highways,
And ******* in the lanes,
You couldn't hear the music
For the rattling of the stones.

The village doctor he was there,
He had his bag of tricks,
And in between the dances
He was sterilizing ******.

Father O'Flanagan he was there,
And in the corner he sat,
Amusing himself by abusing himself
And catching it in his hat.

There was ******* in the couches,
There was ******* in the cots,
And lying up against the wall
Were rows of grinning *****.

Farmer Brown he was there,
A-jumping on his hat,
For half an acre of his corn
Was fairly ******* flat.

Giles he played a dirty trick,
We canna let it pass,

He showed a lass his mighty *****
Then shoved it up her ****.

Bayard Stockton he was there,
Drunk beyond a doubt,
He tried to stuff the parson's wife
But couldna get the root.

Dino's had an even stroke,
His skill was much admired,
He gratified one **** a time,
Until his skill expired.

Lindsay Bedogni he was there,
And he was in despair,
He couldna get his ***** through
The tangles of the hair.

Jockie Stewart did his *******
Right upon the moor,
It was, he thought, much better
Than ******* on the floor.

Jock McVenning he was there,
A-looking for a ****,
But every **** was occupied
And he was out of luck.

Mike McMurdock when he got there,
His ***** was long and high,
But when he'd ****** her forty times
He was ******* mighty dry.

McTavish, oh, yes, he was there,
His ***** was long and broad,
And when he'd ****** the furrier's wife
She had to be rebored.

McCardew-Roberts he was there,
His ***** was all alert,
But when half the night was done
'Twas dangling in the dirt.

The chimney sweep he was there,
They had to throw him out,
For every time he passed his wind
The room was filled with soot.

The doctor's daughter she was there,
She went to gather sticks,
She couldna find a blade of grass
For ***** and standing ******.

The village builder he was there,
He brought his bag of tricks,
He poured cement in all the holes,
And blunted all the ******.

Little Jimmy he was there,
The leader of the choir,
He hit the ***** of all the boys,
To make their voices higher.

Now little Tommy he was there,
But he was only eight,

He couldna root the women,
So he had to masturbate.

The village postman he was there,
The poor man had the pox,
He couldna **** the lassies
So he ****** the letterbox.

The village idiot he was there
A-leaning on the gate,
He couldna find a ****
So he had to flatulate.

The blacksmith's father he was there,
A-roaring like a lion,
He'd cut his **** off in the forge,
So he used a red hot iron.

And when the ball was over
Everyone confessed,
They all enjoyed the dancing
But the ******* was the best.

And so the ball was over
They all went home to rest,
And the music had been exquisite,
But the ******* was the best.

ONCE THERE WAS A SERVANT GIRL
WHOSE NAME WAS MARY JANE

Once there was a servant girl
whose name was Mary Jane,
Her mistress she was good to her
She knew she was a country girl,
just lately from the farm,
And so she did her bloody best
to keep the girl from harm.

Chorus : Singing bell-bottom trousers,
coats of navy blue
Let him climb the rigging
like his Daddy used to do.

The forty-second Army Corps
came in to paint the town,
A band of bawdy bastards
and rapists of renown,
They busted every maidenhead,
and staggered out again,
But they never made the servant girl
who lived in Drury Lane.

Next there came the Fusiliers,
and a band of Welsh Hussars
They piled into the brothels,
they packed into the bars.
The maidens and the matrons
were seduced with might and main,
But they never made the servant girl
whose name was Mary Jane.

Early one evening a sailor came to tea
And that was the start of all her misery,
At sea without a woman
for forty months or more,
There wasn't any need to ask
what he was looking for.

He asked her for a candle
to light his way to bed,
He asked her for a pillow
to rest his weary head,
Then using very gentle words,
as if he meant no harm
He asked the maid to come to bed
just to keep him warm.

She lifted up the covers
just a moment there to lie,
But he's got his **** inside her
before she could bat an eye,
And though he'd got her maidenhead
she showed no great alarm,
And the only words she said to him were:
"I hope you're keeping warm."

Early in the morning
when the sailor'd had his grind
He gave to her a ten bob note
to pacify his mind
Saying: "If you have a daughter
bounce her on your knee,

If you have a son
send the bastard out to sea."

Now all you servant girls
take a warning from me,
Don't ever let a sailor
get an inch above the knee,
She trusted one, the ninny,
in his Naval uniform,
Now all she wants to do, me boys,
is keep the Navy warm.

THE MINSTRELS SING OF A BASTARD KING OF MANY LONG YEARS AGO

The minstrels sing of a Bastard King
of many long years ago
Who ruled his land with an iron hand,
Though his mind was weak and low,
His only outer garment
was a dirty yellow shirt
With which he tried to hide his hide,
But he couldn't hide the dirt.

Chorus: He was forty, fat and full of fleas,
His sceptre sat between his knees,
God bless the Bastard
King of England.

Now the Queen of Spain
was an amorous dame,
And a sprightly wench was she
And longed to play in a sexual way
With the King across the sea.
So she sent a secret message
With a secret messenger
To ask the King if he would string
Along to sleep with her.

Now Ol' Philip of France
he heard by chance
Within his royal court,
And he swore, "By God, she loves this slob
Because I'm rather short,"
So he sent the Duke of Suffering Sap
To give to the Queen a dose of clap
To pass it on to the
Bastard King of England.

When news of the foul deed was heard
Within fair London's walls
The King he swore by the Royal Whore
He'd have King Philip's life.
He offered half the royal purse
And a piece of Princess Claire
To any British subject
Who'd undo Philip the Fair.

The Duke of Northumberland
saddled his horse
And galloped off to France,
He swore he was a fairy,
The King let drop his pants,
Then in front of a throng
he slipped on a thong
Leaped on his horse and galloped along
Dragging the Frenchman back
to Merrie Old England.

When the King of England saw the sight
He fell in a faint on the floor,
For during the ride his rival's hide
Was stretched a yard or more,
And all the whores in silken drawers
Came down to London town,

And shouted round the battlements,
"To Hell with the British Crown."
And Philip alone usurped the throne
His sceptre was his royal bone,
With which he ditched
The Bastard King of England

WHO'S THAT KNOCKING AT MY DOOR?

Who's that knocking at my door?
Cried the fair young maiden.
Oh, it's only me from across the sea,
Cried Barnacle Bill the sailor.

Why are you knocking at my door?
Cried the fair young maiden.
'Cos I'm young enough, and ready and tough,
Cried Barnacle Bill the Sailor.

You can sleep upon the floor.
Oh, get off the floor, you dirty old whore.

You can sleep upon the mat.
Oh, bugger the mat you can't **** that.

You can sleep upon the stairs.
Oh, ****** the stairs they haven't got hairs.

You can sleep between my ****.
Oh, bugger your **** they give me the *****.

You can sleep between my thighs.
Oh, bugger your thighs they're covered in flies.

You can sleep within my ****.
Oh, bugger your **** but I'll **** for a
    stunt.

What will we do when the baby's born?
Oh, we'll drown the bugger and **** for
    another.

I'M A GENTLEMAN OF LEISURE, OF NOBILITY AND PLEASURE

I'm a gentleman of leisure,
of nobility and pleasure,
With manners of the manor
and the morals of the barn,
And when I met a lady
in the forest green and shady,
I asked if I could spin her ball of yarn.

Chorus: Ball of yarn, ball of yarn,
I've a mind to spin
your little ball of yarn,
Ball of yarn, ball of yarn,
I've a mind to spin
your little ball of yarn.

She gave her kind consent
and behind the bush we went,
And I said: "My dear,
there's no cause for alarm."
So I laid her on the ground
and with expertise so sound
I went on to spin her little ball of yarn.

It was nine months after
that in my manor where I sat,
I saw a figure coming past the barn,
And a big man with a truncheon
quite disturbed my Sunday luncheon,
I was father of a little ball of yarn.

DINAH

A rich girl has a limousine
A poor girl has a truck
But the only time that Dinah rides
Is when she has a ****.

Chorus: Dinah, Dinah, show us your leg,
        show us your leg,
        show us your leg,
        Dinah, Dinah, show us your leg,
        A yard above your knee.

A rich girl has a brassière,
A poor girl uses string,
But Dinah uses nothing at all
She lets the bastards swing.

A rich girl has a ring of gold,
A poor girl has one of brass,
But the only ring that Dinah has
Is the one around her ****.

A rich girl uses Vaseline,
A poor girl uses lard,
But Dinah uses axle-grease
Because her ****'s so hard.

A rich girl uses a sanitary towel,
A poor girl uses a sheet,
But Dinah uses nothing at all,
Leaves a trail along the street.

DIAMOND LILY

Oh her name is Diamond Lily
She's a whore in Piccadilly,
And her brother has a brothel in the Strand,
Her father sells his ****hole
At the Elephant and Castle,
They're the richest ******* family
in the land.

There's a man deep in a dungeon
With his hand upon his *****
And the shadow of his ***** upon the wall,
And the ladies as they pass
Stick their hat-pins up his ****,
And the little mice play billiards
with his *****.

There's a little green urinal
To the north of Waterloo
And another a little further up,
There's a member of the army
Playing tunes upon his ****
While the passers by put pennies in his cup.

The doggies held a meeting,
They came from near and far,
Some came by motor-cycle,
Some by motor-car.
Each doggy passed the entrance,
Each doggy signed the book,
Then each unshipped his ****hole
And hung it on the hook.

One dog was not invited,
It sorely raised his ire,
He ran into the meeting hall
And loudly bellowed, "Fire."
It threw them in confusion
And without a second look,
Each grabbed another's ****hole,
From off another hook.

And that's the reason why, sir,
When walking down the street,
And that's the reason why, sir,
When doggies chance to meet,
And that's the reason why, sir,
On land or sea or foam,
He will sniff another's ****hole
To see if it's his own.

CLEMENTINE

There she stood beside the bar rail
Drinking pink gins for two bits,
And the swollen whiskey barrels
Stood in awe beside her tits.

Chorus: I owe my darlin', I owe my darlin'
I owe my darlin' Clementine.
Three bent pennies and a nickel
Oh, my darlin' Clementine.

Eyes of whiskey, lips of water
As she sodden at me peer
Dawns the daylight in her temple
With a *******-warming leer.

Hung me guitar on the bar rail
At the sweetness of the sign,
In one leap leapt out me trousers
Plunged into the foaming brine.

She was bawdy, she was busty,
She could match the great Buzoom,
As she strained out of her bloomers
Like a melon tree in bloom.

Oh the oak tree and the cypress
Never more together twine,
Since that creeping poison ivy
Laid its blight on Clementine.

THE CHASTITY BELT

O pray, gentle maiden,
Let me be your lover,
Condemn me no longer
To mourn and to weep,
Struck down like a hart
I lie bleeding and panting
Let down your drawbridge
I'll enter your keep.
Enter your keep, nonny nonny,
Enter your keep, nonny nonny,
Let down your drawbridge, I'll enter your keep.

Alas, gentle errant,
I am not a maiden,
I'm married to Sir Oswald,
The cunning old Celt,
He's gone to the wars
For a twelve month or longer
And taken the key
To my chastity belt.

Fear not, gentle maiden
For I know a locksmith.
To his forge we will go,
On his door we will knock
And try to avail us
Of his specialized knowledge
And see if he's able
To unpick your lock.

Alas, sir and madam,
To help I'm unable,
My technical knowledge
It is of no avail.
I can't find the secret
Of your combination
The cunning old bastard
Has fitted a Yale.

I'm back from the wars
With sad news of disaster,
A terrible mishap
I have to confide,
As my ship was a-passing
The straits of Gibraltar
I carelessly dropped the key
Over the side.

Alas and alack, I am locked up forever
Then up stepped the page-boy
Saying leave this to me.
If you will allow me
To enter your chamber
I'll open it up with
My duplicate key.

CATS ON THE ROOFTOP

When you wake up in the morning
with the devil of a stand,
From the pressure of the liquid
on the seminary gland,
If you haven't got a woman
use your own horny hand,
As you revel in the joys of masturbation.

Chorus: Singing: Cats on the rooftop,
cats on the tiles,
Cats with the clap
and cats with piles,
*Cats with their *****
wreathed in smiles
As they revel in the joys
of fornication.

The Regimental Sergeant Major
leads a miserable life,
He can't afford a mistress,
and he doesn't have a wife,
So he puts it up the bottom
of the Regimental Fife,
As he revels in the joys of fornication.

When you find yourself in springtime
with a surge of sexual joy,
And your wife has got the rags on,
and your daughter's rather coy,

Then jam it up the jacksie
of your favourite choirboy,
As you revel in a smooth ejaculation.

Long-legged curates grind like goats,
Pale-faced spinsters shag like stoats,
And the whole damn world
stands by and gloats,
As they revel in the joys of fornication.

The ostrich in the desert is a solitary chick,
Without the opportunity to dip its wick,
But whenever it does, it slips in thick,
As he revels in the joys of fornication.

The ape is small and rather slow,
Erect he stands a foot or so,
So when he comes it's time to go,
As he revels in the joys of fornication.

The flea disports among the trees,
And there consorts with whom he please,
To fill the land with bastard fleas,
As he revels in the joy of fornication.

The elephant's **** is big and round,
A small one scales a thousand pound,
Two together rock the ground
As they revel in the joys of fornication.

The camel likes to have his fun,
His night is made when he is done,
He always gets two humps for one,
As he revels in the joys of fornication.

The donkey is a lonely bloke,
He hardly ever gets a poke,
But when he does he lets it soak,
As he revels in the joys of fornication.

The orang-utan is a colourful sight
There's a glow on its arse like a pilot light,
As it jumps and it leaps in the night,
As it revels in the joys of fornication.

The hippopotamus, so it seems,
Very, very rarely has wet dreams,
But when he does he comes in streams,
As he revels in the joys of fornication.

The oyster is a paragon of purity,
And you can't tell the he from the she,
But he can tell and so can she,
As they revel in the joys of fornication.

A thousand verses all in rhyme,
To sit and sing them seems a crime,
When we could better spend our time
Revelling in the joys of fornication.

ESKIMO NELL

Gather round all you whorey
Gather round and hear this story.

When a man grows old
*and his ***** grow cold*
*And the tip of his ***** turns blue,*
And it bends in the middle
Like a one-string fiddle
he can tell you a tale or two.

So pull up a chair, and stand me a drink
And a tale to you I'll tell
Of Dead-eye Dick and Mexican Pete,
And a harlot called Eskimo Nell.

When Dead-eye Dick and Mexican Pete
Go forth in search of fun
*It's Dead-eye Dick that slings the ******
And Mexican Pete the gun.

When Dead-eye Dick and Mexican Pete
Are sore, depressed and sad
*It's always a **** that bears the brunt*
But the shooting ain't so bad.

Now Dead-eye Dick and Mexican Pete
Lived down by Dead Man's Creek
*And such was their luck they'd had no ****
For nigh on half a week.

Just a moose or two and a caribou,
And a bison cow or so,
And for Dead-eye Dick
with his kingly *****
This ******* was mighty slow.

So do or dare this horny pair
Set forth for the Rio Grande,
Dead-eye Dick with his mighty *****
And Pete with his gun in his hand.

And as they blazed their noisy trail
No man their path withstood,
And many a bride, her husband's pride
A pregnant widow stood.

They reached the strand of the Rio Grande
At the height of a blazing noon,
And to slake their thirst and do their worst
They sought Black Mike's Saloon.

And as they pushed the great doors wide
Both ***** and gun flashed free.
"According to sex, you bleeding wrecks,
You drink or **** with me."

They'd heard of the *****
called Dead-eye Dick,
From the Maine to Panama
And with scarcely worse
than a muttered curse
Those dagos sought the bar.

The girls too knew his playful ways
Down on the Rio Grande,
And forty whores
pulled down their drawers
At Dead-eye Dick's command.

They saw the fingers of Mexican Pete
Itch on the trigger grip
And they didn't wait, at fearful rate
Those whores began to strip.

Now Dead-eye Dick was breathing quick
With lecherous snorts and grunts
So forty ***** were bared to view
And likewise forty *****.

Now forty ***** and forty *****
If you can use your wits,
And if you're slick at arithmetic,
Makes exactly eighty tits.

Now eighty tits are a gladsome sight
For a man with a raging stand
It may be rare in Berkeley Square
But not on the Rio Grande.

Now Dead-eye Dick had ****** a few
On the last preceding night,
This he had done just to show his fun
And to whet his appetite.

His phallic limb was in ******* trim,
As he backed and took a run
He made a dart at the nearest tart
And scored a hole in one.

He bore her to the sandy floor
And there he ****** her fine
And though she grinned
It put the wind up the other thirty-nine.

When Dead-eye Dick lets loose his *****
He's got no time to spare,
For speed and length
combined with strength
He fairly singes hair.

He made a dart at the next spare tart,
When into that Harlot's Hell
Strode a gentle maid who was unafraid,
And her name it was Eskimo Nell.

By this time Dick had got his *****
Well into number two
When Eskimo Nell let out a yell,
She bawled to him: "Hey you."

He gave a flick of his muscular *****
And the girl flew over his head,
And he wheeled about with an angry shout.
His face and his ***** were red.

She glanced our hero up and down,
His looks she seemed to decry,
With utter scorn she glimpsed the horn
That rose from his hairy thigh.

She blew the smoke from her cigarette
Over his steaming ****
So utterly beat was Mexican Pete
He failed to do his job.

It was Eskimo Nell who broke the spell
In accents clear and cool:
"You **** struck shrimp
of a Yankee pimp.
You call that thing a ****?"
"If this here town can't take that down,"
She sneered to those cowering whores,
"There's one little **** can do the stunt,
It's Eskimo Nell's, not yours."

She stripped her garments one by one
With an air of conscious pride
And as she stood in her womanhood
They saw the great divide.

She seated herself on a table top
Where someone had left his glass,
With a twitch of her tits
she crushed it to bits
Between the cheeks of her ****.

She flexed her knees with supple ease,
And spread her legs apart,
With a friendly nod to the mangy sod
She gave him the cue to start.

But Dead-eye Dick knew a trick or two,
He meant to take his time,
And a girl like this was ******* bliss
So he played the pantomime.

He flexed his ****hole to and fro
And made his ***** inflate
Until they looked like granite knobs
On top of a garden gate.

He blew his anus inside out,
His ***** increased in size,
His mighty ***** grew twice as thick
Till it almost reached his eyes.

He polished it up with alcohol,
And made it steaming hot
To finish the job he sprinkled the knob
With a cayenne pepperpot.

Then neither did he take a run
Nor did he take a leap,
Nor did he stoop, but took a swoop
And a steady forward creep.

With piercing eye he took a sight
Along his mighty ****,
And the steady grin as he pushed it in
Was calculatedly cool.

Have you seen the giant pistons
On the mighty C.P.R.,
With the driving force of a thousand horse
Well, you know what pistons are.

Or you think you do. But you've yet to learn
The ins and outs of the trick
Of the work that's done on a non-stop run
By a guy like Dead-eye Dick.

But Eskimo Nell was no infidel,
As good as a whole harem
With the strength of ten in her abdomen
And the rock of ages between.

Amid stops she could take the stream
Like the flush of a watercloset,
And she gripped his ****
like a Chatswood Lock
On the National Safe Deposit.

But Dead-eye Dick could not come quick,
He meant to conserve his powers,
If he'd a mind he'd grind and grind
For a couple of solid hours.

Nell lay for a while with a subtle smile,
The grip of her **** grew keener,
With a squeeze of her thigh
she sucked him dry
With the ease of a vacuum cleaner.

She performed this trick in a way so slick
As to set in complete defiance
The basic cause and primary laws
That govern sexual science.

She calmly rode through the phallic code
Which for years had stood the test,
And the ancient rules of the Classic schools
In a second or two went West.

And so my friends we come to the end
Of copulation's classic
The effect on Dick was sudden and quick
And akin to an anaesthetic.

He fell to the floor and knew no more,
His passions extinct and dead,
And he did not shout as his ***** fell out
Though 'twas stripped
right down to a thread.

Then Mexican Pete jumped to his feet
To avenge his pal's affront,
With jarring jolt of his blue-nosed Colt
He rammed it up her ****.

He rammed it up to the trigger grip
And fired three times three
But to his surprise she closed her eyes
And smiled in ecstasy.

She jumped to her feet with a smile so sweet
"Bully", she said, "for you.
Though I might have guessed
that that was the best
That you two poor ***** could do.
"When next, my friend, that you intend
To sally forth for fun
Buy Dead-eyed Dick a sugar stick
And yourself an elephant gun."

" I'm going back to the frozen North,
Where the ****** are hard and strong
Back to the land of the frozen stand
Where the nights are six months long.

"It's hard as tin when they put it in
In the land where spunk is spunk
Not a trickling stream of lukewarm cream
But a solid frozen chunk.

"Back to the land where they understand
What it means to fornicate,
Where even the dead sleep two in a bed
And the babies masturbate.

"Back to the land of the grinding gland,
Where the walrus plays with his prong,
Where the polar bear wanks off in his lair
That's where they'll sing this song.

"They'll tell this tale on the Arctic trail
Where the nights are sixty below,
Where it's so damn cold
that the Johnnies are sold
Wrapped up in a ball of snow.

"In the valley of death with baited breath
That's where they'll sing it too,
Where the skeletons rattle in sexual battle,
And the rotting corpses screw.

"Back to the land where men are men,
Terra Bellicum,
And there I'll spend my worthy end
For the North is calling: 'Come'."

So Dead-eye Dick and Mexico Pete
Slunk out of the Rio Grande,
Dead-eye Dick with his useless *****
And Pete with no gun in his hand.

A verse of appreciation:
When a man grows old
And his ***** go cold
And the end of his **** turns blue
And the hole in the middle
Refuses to piddle,
I'd say he was ******, wouldn't you?

DUREX IS A GIRL'S BEST FRIEND

A poke with a bloke may be quite incidental,
Durex is a girl's best friend,
You may get the works
But you won't be parental.
As he slides it in,
You trust that good old latex skin
As he lets fly, none gets by
'Cos it's all gathered up in the end.
This little precaution
Avoids an abortion
Durex is a girl's best friend.

DO YOURS HANG LOW?

Do your ***** hang low,
Do they dangle to and fro,
Can you tie them in a knot,
Can you tie them in a bow,
Can you sling 'em o'er your shoulder
Like a continental soldier,
Do your ***** hang low?

DON'T SAY NO

Oh, my darling, don't say no,
Onto the sofa you must go.
Up with your petticoat,
Down with your drawers,
You tickle mine
And I'll tickle yours.

FANNY BAY

If you ever go across the sea to Darwin,
Then maybe at the closing of the day,
You will see the local harlots
at their business,
And watch the sun go down on Fanny Bay.

Some are black and some are white,
And some are brindle,
And some are young
and some are old and grey,
But what will cost you twenty quid
in Lower Crown Street,
Will cost you half a zac in Fanny Bay.

THE GOOD SHIP VENUS

'Twas on the good ship Venus,
My God you should 'av seen us,
The figurehead was a nude in bed
Sucking a red-hot *****.

Chorus: Frigging in the rigging,
Wanking on the planking,
Masturbating on the grating
There was **** all else to do.

The captain's name was Slugger
He was a dirty bugger
He wasn't fit to shovel ****
On any bugger's lugger.

The first mate's name was Paul,
He only had one ****,
But with that cracker he rolled terbaccer
Around the cabin wall.

The second mate's name was Andy
His ***** were long and bandy,
They filled his **** with molten brass
For pissing in the brandy.

The third mate's name was Morgan,
He was a grisly Gorgon,
Three times a day he strummed away
Upon his sexual organ.

The captain's wife was Mabel
And whenever she was able
She gave the crew their Daily Screw
Upon the messroom table.

The Captain's randy daughter
Was swimming in the water,
Delighted squeals came as the eels
Entered her sexual quarter.

A cook whose name was Freeman,
He was a dirty demon,
He fed the crew on menstrual stew
And hymens fried in semen.

Another cook was O'Malley,
He didn't dilly dally,
He shot his bolt with such a jolt
He whitewashed half the galley.

The Boatswain's name was Lester,
He was a hymen tester,
Through hymens thick he shoved his *****
And left it there to fester.

The engineer was McTavish
And young girls he did ravish,
His missing ****'s at Istanbul
He was a trifle lavish.

A homo was the Purser,
He couldn't have been worser,
With all the crew he had a screw,
Until they yelled: "Oh no sir."

Another one was Cropper
Oh Christ he had a whopper,
Twice round the deck
Once round his neck
And up his bum for a stopper.

The cabin boy was Kipper,
A dirty little nipper,
They stuffed his **** with broken glass
And circumcised the skipper.

The ship's dog's name was Rover
The whole crew did him over,
They ground and ground the faithful hound
From Singapore to Dover.

'Twas in the Adriatic
Where the water's almost static
The rise and fall of **** and ****
Was almost automatic.

The end of this narration
Came in jubilation,
For they sunk the junk in a sea of spunk,
Caused by masturbation.

So now we end this serial
Through sheer lack of material,
I wish you luck and freedom from
Diseases venereal.

Three German officers crossed the line,
Parlez-vous,
Three German officers crossed the line,
Parlez-vous,
Three German officers crossed the line
*They ****** the women*
and drank the wine,
Inky, pinky, parlez-vous.

They came upon a wayside inn,
***** on the mat and walked right in.*

Oh landlord have you a daughter fair,
Lily-white tits and golden hair?

At last they got her on a bed
Shagged her till her cheeks were red.

And then they took her to a shed,
Shagged her till she was nearly dead.

They took her down a shady lane,
Shagged her back to life again.

They shagged her up, they shagged her down,
They shagged her right round the town.

They shagged her in, they shagged her out,
They shagged her up her waterspout.

Seven months went and all was well,
Eight months went and she started to swell.

Nine months went, she gave a grunt,
And a little white bastard popped out of
    her ****.

The little white bugger he grew and grew
He shagged his mother and sister too.

The little white bugger he went to hell,
He shagged the Devil and his wife as well.

GENTLEMEN SHOULD PLEASE REFRAIN

Gentlemen should please refrain
From flushing toilets while the train
Is standing in the station for a while.
We encourage contemplation
While the train is in the station,
Cross your legs and grit your teeth and smile.

If you wish to pass some water
You should sing out for a porter
Who will place a basin in the bog;
Tramps and hoboes underneath
Get it in the eye and teeth,
But that's what comes from being underdog.

Drinking while the train is moving
Is another way of proving,
That control of eye and hand is sure;
We like our clients to be neat,
So please don't wet upon the seat,
Or, even worse, don't splash upon the floor.

If the Ladies' Room be taken,
do not feel the least forsaken,
Never show the sign of sad defeat,
Try the Gents across the hall,
and if some man has felt the call
He'll courteously relinquish you his seat.

If these efforts are in vain,
then simply break the window pane,
This novel method's used by very few,
We go strolling through the park,
a-goosing statues in the dark
If Peter Pan can take it, why can't you?

THE HARLOT OF JERUSALEM

In the days of old there lived a maid,
She was the mistress of her trade,
A prostitute of high repute
The harlot of Jerusalem.

Chorus: Hi ho Cathusalem,
          Cathusalem, Cathusalem
          Hi ho Cathusalem,
          Harlot of Jerusalem.

And though she ****** for many a year
Of pregnancy she had no fear,
She washed her passage out with beer,
The best in all Jerusalem.

Now in a hovel by the wall
A student lived with but one ****,
Who'd been through all, or nearly all
The harlots of Jerusalem.

His phallic limb was lean and tall
His phallic art caused all to fall
And victims lined the Wailing Wall
That goes around Jerusalem.

One night returning from a spree
With customary whore-lust he
Made up his mind to call and see
The harlot of Jerusalem.

It was for her no fortune good,
That he should need to root his pud,
And chose her out of all the brood
Of harlots of Jerusalem.

For though he paid his women well,
This syphilitic spawn of hell,
Struck down each year and tolled the bell
For ten harlots of Jerusalem.

Forth from the town he took the slut,
For 'twas his whim always to rut,
By the Salvation Army hut
Outside of Old Jerusalem.

With artful eye and leering look,
He took out from its filthy nook,
His organ twisted like a crook
The Pride of Old Jerusalem.

He leaned the whore against the slum
And tied her at the knee and bum,
Knowing where the strain would come,
Upon the fair Cathusalem.

He seized the harlot by the bum,
And rattling like a Lewis gun,
He sowed the seed of many a son
Into the fair Cathusalem.

It was a sight to make you sick
To hear him grunt so fast and quick
While rending with his crooked *****
The womb of fair Cathusalem.

Then up there came an Onanite,
With warty ***** besmeared with ****,
He'd sworn that he would gaol that night
The harlot of Jerusalem.

He loathed the act of copulation,
For his delight was masturbation,
And with a spurt of cruel elation
He saw the whore Cathusalem.

So when he saw the grunting pair,
With roars of rage he rent the air,
And vowed that he would soon take care
Of the harlot of Jerusalem.

Upon the earth he found a stick
To which he fastened half a brick
And took a swipe at the mighty *****
Of the student of Jerusalem.

He seized the bastard by his crook,
Without a single furious look
And flung him over Kedron's brook
That babbles past Jerusalem.

The student gave a furious roar
And rushed to even up the score,

And with his swollen **** did bore
The **** of Cathusalem.

And reeling full of rage and fight
He pushed the bastard Onanite,
And rubbed his face in Cathy's ****,
The foulest in Jerusalem.

Cathusalem she knew her part
She closed her **** and blew a fart,
That sent him flying like a dart,
Right over old Jerusalem.

And buzzing like a bumble bee
He flew straight out towards the sea,
But caught his ****hole in a tree
That grows in old Jerusalem.

And to this day you still can see
His ****hole hanging from that tree,
Let that to you a warning be
When passing through Jerusalem.

And when the moon is bright and red,
A castrated form sails overhead,
Still raining curses on the head
Of the harlot of Jerusalem.

As for the student and his lass,
Many a playful night did pass,
Until she joined the V.D. class
For harlots in Jerusalem.

I DON'T WANT TO JOIN THE ARMY

I don't want to join the army,
I don't want to go to war,
I just want to hang around
Piccadilly Underground,
Living on the earnings of a high class lady.
I don't need no Froggy women,
London's full of girls I never 'ad,
I want to stay in Blighty
Lord Gawd Almighty,
Following in the footsteps of me Dad.

Chorus: Call up the buggers
in the Royal Marines,
Call up the Queen's Artillery
Call up me brother,
me sister and me mother
But for Gawd's sake don't call me.

Monday night me 'and was on her ankle,
Tuesday night me 'and was on her thigh,
Wednesday night, hooray,
I pulled her pants away,
Thursday night I felt that I
was really getting high,
Friday night I got me hand upon it,
Saturday gave it just a little tweak,
Sunday after dinner I finally got it in 'er,
And now I'm paying thirty bob a week,
Gorblimey.

I don't want to join the Navy,
I don't want to go to sea,
I just want to go
Down to old Soho
Tickling all the girlies
in the umtiddly-um-pum.
*I don't want a bayonet up my ****hole,*
I don't want me knackers shot away,
I'd rather live in England,
Merry, Merry England,
And fornicate my living days away.

KNOBBY HALL

Oh, his name was Knobby Hall,
Knobby Hall,
Oh, his name was Knobby Hall,
Knobby Hall,
Oh, his name was Knobby Hall,
*And he only had one ****,*
*But 'twas better than **** all,*
Damn his eye, blast his soul,
********* hell, ****.*

Yes, his name was Knobby Hall,
Though he only had one ball,
The other one was hanging on the wall,
Damn his eye . . .

They say he stabbed his wife,
But it wasn't with a knife,
No, it wasn't with a knife,
Damn his eye . . .

Oh, the preacher he did come,
And he looked so bloody glum,
He can kiss my bloody ***,
Damn his eye . . .

Oh, the judge's name was Dreck.
Said, "You killed her with your *****,
We shall stretch your ******* neck,
Damn your eyes . . ."

To the gallows I must go,
And those buggers down below
Think it's all a bloody show,
Damn their eyes . . .

I saw Lily in the crowd,
And I hollered right out loud,
"**** you, Lily, aint yer proud,
Damn your eyes . . ."

Well the hangman's name was Goose,
Had a **** so long and loose,
That he used it as a noose,
Damn his eyes.

Now in heaven I do dwell,
And I'm feeling bloody ill,
For the whores are down in hell,
Damn their eyes . . .

THE KEYHOLE IN THE DOOR

I was invited for the weekend
to a ball at Cholmondely Hall,
To celebrate the wedding
of Sue Vere and Cousin Paul.
I read the guest list over
and imagine my delight,
When I found Sweet Fanny Adams
had come to spend the night.

Chorus: *Oh, the keyhole in the door,*
         the door,
           The keyhole in the door,
           I took up my position
           by the keyhole in the door.

The ball was one of splendour,
all the city nobs were there,
Touching up the ladies
like farmers at the fair,
And Fanny fairly dazzled
as she danced around the floor,
I resolved to be lie in wait for her
by the keyhole in the door.

I left the ballroom early,
just after half-past nine,
And as I hoped to find it
her room lay next to mine,

So taking off my trousers I set off to explore
And took up my position
by the keyhole in the door.

I hadn't long to wait there
wrapped in my dressing gown,
When I saw Fanny on the staircase,
retiring all alone,
She didn't lock her bedroom door
I couldn't ask for more,
And I crept out of the shadows
by the keyhole in the door.

First she removed her stockings,
her silken legs to show,
And then her frilly panties
to reveal her furbelow,
"Now take off all the other things,"
was all I could implore,
And silently I gripped the knob
and crossed the threshold door.

Silently I shut the door
and took her in my arms,
And sooner than I'd expected,
discovered all her charms,
And in case another person
should see the sights I saw,
I hung her frilly panties
o'er the keyhole in the door.

That night I rode in glory
as I plumbed the girl's insides
And on her heaving belly
I had many splendid rides,
But when I woke next morning
my **** was red and sore,
And I felt that I'd been screwing
through the keyhole in the door.

JOHN PEEL

Do you ken John Peel
With his ***** of steel
And his ***** of brass
And his celluloid ****,
Do you ken John Peel
With his ***** of steel
And it all comes out in the morning.

JACK AND JILL

Jack and Jill went up the hill
To fetch a pail of water.
Jill came down with half a crown
But not for fetching water.

INSIDE THOSE RED PLUSH BREECHES

John Thomas was a servant tall
Pride and joy of the servants' hall,
Although he only had one ****,
Inside his red plush breeches.

Chorus: Inside those red plush breeches,
Inside those red plush breeches,
Inside those red plush breeches,
That kept John Thomas warm.

Of all the servants at the servants' post,
Mary was the one he loved the most,
And she'd keep her hands as warm as toast,
Inside his red plush breeches.

Mary had an illigit
***** green and face like ****,
And every time she looked at it,
She cursed those red plush breeches.

Now Mary laid poor John a trap,
And he fell for it like a sap,
And now he's got a dose of clap,
Inside those red plush breeches.

IVAN SCAVINSKY SCAVAR

The harems of Egypt are fine to behold,
The harlots the fairest of fair,
But the fairest of all was owned by a sheik
Named Abdul Abulbul Emir.

A travelling brothel
came down from the North,
'Twas run privately for the Tsar,
Who wagered a hundred no one could outshag
Ivan Scavinsky Scavar.

A day was arranged for the spectacle great,
A holiday proclaimed by the Tsar,
And the streets were all lined
with the harlots assigned
To Ivan Scavinsky Scavar.

Old Abdul came in
with a snatch by his side,
His eye bore a leer of desire,
And he started to brag
how he would out shag
Ivan Scavinsky Scavar.

All hairs they were shorn,
no frenchies were worn,
And this suited Abdul by far,
And he's quite set his mind
on a fast action grind
To beat Ivan Scavinsky Scavar.

They met on the track
with ***** at the slack
A starter's gun punctured the air,
They were both quick to rise,
the crowd gaped at the size
Of Abdul Abulbul Emir.

They worked all the night
in the pale yellow light,
Old Abdul he revved like a car,
But he couldn't compete
with the slow steady beat
Of Ivan Scavinsky Scavar.

So Ivan he won and he shouldered his gun,
He bent down to polish the pair,
When something red hot
up his back passage shot
'Twas Abdul Abulbul Emir.

The harlots turned green,
the crowd shouted "Queen,"
They were ordered apart by the Tsar,
'Twas bloody bad luck for Abdul was stuck
Up Ivan Scavinsky Scavar.

The cream of the joke came when they broke,
'Twas laughed at for years by the Tsar,
For Abdul the fool left half his ****
Up Ivan Scavinsky Scavar.

She was poor but she was honest
Victim of a rich man's whim,
First he ****** her, then he left her,
And she had a child by him.

Chorus : It's the same the whole world over
It's the poor wot gets the blame,
It's the rich gets all the pleasure,
Ain't it all a bleeding' shame.

See him with his hounds and horses,
See him strutting at his club,
While the victim of his whoring
Drinks her gin inside a pub.

Then she came to London city
Just to hide her bleeding shame,
But a Labour leader ****** her,
Put her on the streets again.

See him in the House of Commons
Passing laws to combat crime,
While the victim of his evil
Walks the streets at night in shame.

See him riding in a carriage
Past the gutter where she stands,
He has made a stylish marriage
While she wrings her ringless hands.

See him sitting at the theatre
In the front row with the best,
While the girl that he has ruined
Entertains a sordid guest.

See her on the bridge at midnight
Throwing snowballs at the moon,
She said, "Jack, I never 'ad it."
But she spoke too ******* soon.

See her on the bridge at midnight
Picking blackheads from her crutch,
She said: "Jack, I never 'ad it."
He said: "No, not ******* much "

See her stand in Piccadilly
Offering her aching ****,
She is now completely ruined
It was all because of him.

See him seated in his Rolls Royce
Driving homeward from the hunt,
He got riches from his marriage,
She got corns upon her ****.

See her on the bridge at midnight
Saying: "Farewell blighted love."
Then a scream, a splash, Oh goodness,
What is she a-doing of?

When they dragged her from the river
Water from her clothes they wrung
And they thought that she was drownded
Till her corpse got up and sung:

Then there came a wealthy pimp,
Marriage was the tale he told,
She had no one else to take her
So she sold her soul for gold.

In a little country cottage
There her grieving parents live,
Though they drink the fizz she sends them
Yet they never will forgive.

THE MONK OF GREAT RENOWN

There was a monk of great renown,
There was a monk of great renown,
There was a monk of great renown,
Who shagged an innocent maid from town.

Chorus: The old sod, the sod,
The bugger deserved to die.

His brother monks they cried in shame,
So he turned her over and shagged her again.

He met another by the mill,
And shagged and shagged her up the hill.

He met another in the hay,
And put her in the family way.

He took her to the abbot's bed,
And shagged and shagged till she was dead.

But when the abbot cried, "Amen,"
He shagged her back to life again.

His brother monks to stop his frolics,
Put a nail through his **** *and cut off*
his ********.

And now the moral I will tell,
And now the moral I will tell,
When all the world just feels like hell,
Just shag and shag till all is well.

THE MAID OF THE MOUNTAIN GLEN

There was a maid of the mountain glen
Seduced herself with a fountain pen.
The pen it broke and the ink ran wild
And she gave birth to a blue-black child.

Chorus: They called the bastard Stephen
           They called the bastard Stephen,
           They called the bastard Stephen,
           For that was the name of the ink
           (Quink, Quink).

Stephen was a bonny child,
Pride and joy of his mother mild,
And all that worried her was this—
His steady stream of blue-black piss.

Mary of New Brighton Pier
Seduced herself with a bottle of beer.
The top came off and the froth ran wild
And she gave birth to a nut brown child.

Chorus: They called the bastard Frellfalls
           They called the bastard Frellfalls
           They called the bastard Frellfalls
           For that was the name of the beer
           (Queer, Queer)

THOSE OLD RED FLANNEL DRAWERS
THAT MAGGIE WORE

They were tattered, they were torn,
Round the crotchpiece they were worn,

Chorus: Those old red flannel drawers
that Maggie wore.

They were hemmed in, they were tucked in,
They were the drawers
that she was married in.

They were rotten down the front
*With the dripping of her ****.*

She put them on the mat,
And paralysed the cat.

She put them in the sink,
My God, there was a stink.

She hung them on the line,
And the sun refused to shine.

She buried them in the ground,
Killed the grass for miles around.

Oh gather round you sailor boys
And listen to my plea,
'Cos when you've heard it you will pity me,
'Cos I was a goddamn fool
In the port of Liverpool,
The first time that I came home from sea.

Chorus: Oh, my darling Maggie May
    They have taken her away,
    And no more down Lime Street
    will she roam
    For the judge he guilty found her
    For robbing a homeward bounder,
    That dirty, robbin',
    no good Maggie May.

I was a sailor bound for home,
All the way from Sierra Leone,
And two pound ten a month
had been my pay,
As I jingled in my tin
I was sadly taken in
By the lady of the name of Maggie May.

When I steered into her
I just hadn't a care
I was cruisin' up and down
Ol' Canning Place.

She was dressed in a gown so fine,
Like a frigate of the line,
And I bein' a sailorman, gave chase.

She gave me a saucy nod,
And I like a farmer's clod
Let her take me line abreast in tow,
And under all plain sail
We ran before the gale
And to the Crow's Nest Tavern
we did go.

Next morning when I awoke,
I found that I was broke.
No trousers, coat or wallet could I find,
And when I asked her where
She said, "My dear young sir,
You'll find them in the pawnshop
number nine."

To the pawnshop I did go,
No trousers could I find,
So the cops they came
and took this girl away.
Oh, you thieving Maggie May,
You robbed me of my pay,
It'll pay your fare right out to Botany Bay.

She was chained and sent away
From Liverpool one day.

The lads they cheered
as she sailed down the bay,
An' every sailor lad
He only was too glad,
They'd sent the old tart out to Botany Bay.

Oh, Maggie, Maggie May
They have taken you away,
For to stay on Van Dieman's cruel shore.
Oh, you robbed many a whaler
And many a drunken sailor,
But you'll never cruise
round Liverpool no more.

POOR LITTLE ANGELINE

She was sweet sixteen on the village green,
Pure and innocent was Angeline,
A virgin still, never known a thrill
Poor little Angeline.

At the village fair the Squire was there
Masturbating on the village square
When he chanced to see the dainty knee
Of poor little Angeline.

Now the village squire had but one desire,
*To be the biggest ******
in the whole dam shire,
He had set his heart on the vital part
Of poor little Angeline.

As she lifted up her skirt to avoid the dirt
She slipped in a puddle
of the Squire's last squirt,
At the sight he saw,
*how his **** grew raw*
For poor little Angeline.

So he raised his hat and said:
"Miss, your cat
Has been run over and is squashed quite flat,
Now my car is in the square
and I'll take you there
Oh poor little Angeline."

Now the filthy old****
should have got the bird
But she climbed right in without a word,
As they drove away
you could hear them say:
"Poor little Angeline."

They had not gone far
when he stopped the car
And took little Angeline into a bar,
Where he gave her gin just to make her sin
Poor little Angeline.

When he'd oiled her well
he took her to a dell
There to give her bloody ******* hell,
And he tried his luck with a low down ****
On poor little Angeline.

With a cry of "Rape" he raised his cape,
Poor little Angeline had no escape,
Now it's time someone came
to save the name
Of poor little Angeline.

Now the village blacksmith
was brave and bold
And had loved little Angeline
for years untold,
And he vowed he'd be true
whatever they'd do
To poor little Angeline.

But sad to say that very same day
The blacksmith had gone to jail to stay
For coming in his pants at the local dance
With poor little Angeline.

Now the window of his cell
overlooked the dell
Where the Squire was giving
little Angeline hell,
And there upon the grass he observed the ****
Of poor little Angeline.

Now he got such a start that he let out a fart
And blew the whole bloody jail apart,
And he ran like ****
lest the Squire should split
His poor little Angeline.

When he got to the spot
and he saw what was what
He tied the villain's *****
in a granny knot,
For there upon the grass
was the imprint of the ****
Of poor little Angeline.

"Oh, blacksmith true, I love you, I do,
And I can tell by your trousers
that you love me too,
Here I am undressed, come and do your best,"
Cried poor little Angeline.

Now it would be wrong here
to end this song
For the blacksmith had a *****
fully one foot long,
And his natural charm
was as thick as your arm
Lucky little Angeline.

LIFE PRESENTS A DISMAL PICTURE

Life presents a dismal picture
Dark and dreary as the womb,
Father's got an anal stricture
Mother's got a fallen womb.

Sister Sue has been aborted
For the forty-second time,
Brother Bill has been deported
For a homosexual crime.

Nurse has chronic menstruation,
Never laughs and never smiles,
Mine's a dismal occupation
Cracking ice for Grandpa's piles.

In a small brown paper parcel
Wrapped in a mysterious way
Is an imitation rectum
Grandad uses twice a day.

Joe the postman called this morning,
Stuck his ***** through the door,
We could not despite endearment
Get it out till half-past four.

Even now the baby's started
Having epileptic fits,
Every time it coughs it spews
Every time it farts it *****.

Yet we are not broken-hearted,
Neither are we up the spout,
Aunty Mabel has just farted,
Blown her ****hole inside out.

The portions of the female
that appeal to man's depravity,
Are fashioned with considerable care,
And what at first appears
to be a modest cavity,
Is really an elaborate affair.
Now doctors who have studied
these feminine phenomena,
With numerous experiments on dames,
Have taken all the items
of the gentle sex's abdomina,
And given them all lengthy Latin names.
There's the Culva, the Vagina,
and of course the old Peronina,
And the Hymen that is often
found in brides,
There's a lot of little things—
you'd love 'em if you see 'em,
The Clitoris and God knows what besides.
What a pity it is then,
that we common people chatter
Of those mysteries to which I have referred,
And we use for such delicate
and omplicated matter,
Such a very short and vulgar little word.
The erudite authorities who study
the geography
Of that obscure but entertaining land,

Are able to indulge a taste
for intricate topography,
And view the happy details close at hand.
But ordinary people though aware
of their existence,
And complexities beneath the public know
Are normally content
just to view them at a distance,
And treat them roughly speaking as a show.
And therefore when we laymen
probe the secrets of virginity,
Our methods are perhaps a little blunt,
We do not cloud the issue
with meticulous Latinity,
But call the whole concern a simple ****.
For men have made this useful
and pleasure-giving article,
The topic of innumerable jibes,
And though the name is odd
which they have given to this particle,
It seems to fit the subject it describes.

O'REILLY'S DAUGHTER

Sitting in O'Reilly's bar
drinking rum and coca cola,
Suddenly there came to mind,
*I'd like to**** O'Reilly's daughter.*

Chorus: Hi yi yi—Hi yi, yi, Hi yi yi,
The one-eyed Reilly,
*Rub it up, stuff it up, ***** and all,*
Play it on your old base drum.

Her hair was black, her eyes were blue,
the colonel and the major
and the captain sought her,
The regimental goat and the drummer boy too,
but they never had a thump with
O'Reilly's daughter.

Jack O'Flannagan is my name,
I'm the king of copulation,
Drinking beer my claim to fame,
shagging women my occupation.

Walking through the town one day,
who should I meet but O'Reilly's daughter,
Not a word to her did say
but don't you think we really oughter.

Quickly up the stairs to bed,
shagged and shagged until I stove her,
Having lost her maidenhead
she laughed like hell when the fun was over.

I ****** her till her tits were flat,
filled her up with soapy water,
She won't get away with that, if she doesn't
have twins then she really oughter.

I hear footsteps on the stairs,
Old Man Reilly bent on slaughter,
With two pistols in his hand
looking for the man who shagged his daughter.

Grabbed O'Reilly by the hair,
shoved his head in a pail of water,
Rammed those pistols up his ****,
damned sight harder than I shagged his daughter.

Come you virgins, maidens fair,
answer me quick and true no slyly,
Do you want it fair and straight and square,
or the way I give it to the one-eyed Reilly.

Old King Cole was a merry old soul,
And a merry old soul was he,
He called for his wife
in the middle of the night,
And he called for his fiddlers three.
Now every fiddler had a very fine fiddle,
And a very fine fiddle had he,
Fiddle diddle dee diddle dee,
said the fiddlers,
What merry merry men are we,
There's none so fair as can compare,
With the boys of the R.F.C.

Old King Cole was a merry old soul,
And a merry old soul was he,
He called for his wife
in the middle of the night,
And he called for his tailors three.
Now every tailor had a very fine needle,
And a very fine needle had he,
Stick it in and out, in and out,
said the tailors,
Fiddle diddle dee diddle dee,
said the fiddlers,
What merry merry men are we,
There's none so fair as can compare,
With the boys of the R.F.C.

Old King Cole was a merry old soul,
And a merry old soul was he,
He called for his wife
in the middle of the night,
And he called for his jugglers three.
Now every juggler
had two very fine balls,
And two very fine balls had he,
Throw your balls in the air,
said the jugglers,
Stick it in and out, in and out,
said the tailors,
Fiddle diddle dee diddle dee,
said the fiddlers,
What merry merry men are we,
There's none so fair as can compare
With the boys of the R.F.C.

The butchers had choppers:
put it on the block, chop it off.
The barmaids had candles:
pull it out, pull it out, pull it out.
The cyclists had pedals:
round and round, round and round.
The flutists had flutes:
root diddly-oot-diddly-oot.
The painters had brushes:
wop it up and down, up and down.
The horsemen had saddles:
ride it up and down, up and down.

The carpenters had hammers:
bang away, bang away, bang away.
The surgeons had knives:
cut it round the knob, make it throb.
The parsons had very great alarm:
goodness gracious me.
The fishermen had rods:
mine is six feet long.
The huntsmen had horns:
wake up in the morn with a horn.
The coalmen had sacks:
want it in the front or the back?

For forty days and forty nights
We sailed the broad Atlantic,
And never to pass a piece of ****,
It drove us nearly frantic.

Chorus: Away, away with fife and drum
           Here we come full of rum
           Lookin' for women who'll peddle
           their ***
           On the North Atlantic Squadron.

The cook she ran around the deck
The Captain he pursued her,
He caught her on the afterdeck
The dirty bastard screwed her.

The cabin boy, the cabin boy,
The dirty little nipper,
He filled his bum with bubble gum,
And vulcanized the skipper.

The Captain loved the cabin boy,
He loved him like a brother,
And every night between the sheets
They cornholed one another.

The second mate did masturbate,
No **** was higher or wider
They cut off his **** upon a rock
For pissing in the cider.

In days of old when knights were bold,
And women weren't particular,
They lined them up against the wall
*And ****** them perpendicular.*

In days of old when men were bold,
And Hohnnies weren't invented,
*They wrapped a sock around their ****
And babies were prevented.

We're off, we're off to Montreal,
*We'll **** the women,*
*we'll **** them all,*
We'll pickle their cherries in alcohol,
On the North Atlantic Squadron.

There was a whore from Montreal,
She spread her legs from wall to wall,
*But all she got was sweet **** all*
From the North Atlantic Squadron.

There was a whore from Singapore
Hung upside down inside a door,
And she was left
Split, worn and sore
By the North Atlantic Squadron.

Come you old drunkards give ear to my tale,
This short little story will make you turn pale,
It's about a young lady—so pretty and small
Who married a man who had no***** at all.

Chorus : *****, *****,
No ***** at all,
She married a man
Who had no ***** at all.

How well she remembered
the night they were wed,
She rolled back the sheets and crept into bed,
She felt for his *****,
how strange, it was small,
She felt for his *****,
he had no ***** at all.

Mommy, oh Mommy, oh pity my luck,
I've married a man who's unable to ****,
His tool bag is empty,
his screwdriver's small,
The impotent wretch has got no nuts at all.

Daughter, my daughter, now don't be a sap,
I had the same trouble with your dear old Pap,

There's many a man who'll come to the call
Of the wife of the man
who's got no ******** at all.

The pretty young girl took her mother's advice
And found the whole thing exceedingly nice,
An eleven-pound baby was born in the fall,
But the poor little bastard
had no ***** at all.

NELLY CARTWRIGHT

Nell was a mountain maid
Who always was afraid,
That a drunken sot might fill her ****,
As she lay sleeping in the shade,
She took her fears in hand

and filled it up with sand
To keep the boys from stolen joys
In Nelly's Promised Land.

Chorus: Oh the moon shines down
on Nelly Cartwright,
She couldn't fart right,
her **** was airtight,
And though she tried
she couldn't start right,
With a knife she'd watched her
Promised Land.

Now there was a trapper wise,
Who sought out Nelly's prize,
With a dead coyoot on the end of his boot,
He made young Nelly open her eyes,
But as soon as she came to life
She reached for her hunting knife,
A flash in the air, a cry of despair,
And she severed his love life.

Oh women if you want to be wives
Put away those knives,

The men might pay for a lay in the hay,
But they're not gonna pay
for the rest of their lives,
My old mother said
if you're lying in your bed,
If you can't get aid, don't reach for a blade,
Have a bloody good **** *instead.*

MY OLD MAN

My old man was a miner,
Worked all day in the pit.
Sometimes he'd shovel up coal dust,
Sometimes he'd shovel up ****.

Chorus: Singing hey jig-a-jig **** a little pig
Follow the band, follow the band,
With your **** in your hand.

My old man is a carpenter,
And a fine carpenter is he.
All day long he screws screws in
And then he comes home and screws me.

My old man is a taxidermist,
And a fine taxidermist is he.
All day long he stuffs animals,
And then he comes home and stuffs me.

My old man is a trumpeter,
And a very fine trumpeter is he.
All day long he blows trumpets,
And then he comes home and blows me.

My father makes book on the corner,
My mother makes illicit gin,
My sister sells kisses to sailors,
My God how the money rolls in.

Chorus: Rolls in, rolls in, my God
how the money rolls in, rolls in
Rolls in, rolls in, my God
how the money rolls in.

My mother's a bawdy house keeper,
Every night when the evening grows dim,
She hangs out a little red lantern,
My God how the money rolls in.

My cousin's a Harley Street surgeon,
With instruments long, sharp and thin,
He only does one operation,
My God how the money rolls in.

Uncle Joe is a registered plumber,
His business in holes and in tin,
He'll plug your hole for a tanner,
My God how the money rolls in.

My brother's a poor missionary,
He saves fallen women from sin,
He'll save you a blonde for a guinea,
My God how the money rolls in.

My Grandad sells cheap prophylactics,
And punctures the teats with a pin,
For Grandma gets rich from abortions,
My God how the money rolls in.

My uncle is carving out candles,
From wax that is surgically soft,
He hopes it'll fill up the gap
If ever his business wears off.

My sister's a barmaid in Sydney,
For a shilling she'll strip to the skin,
She's stripping from morning to midnight,
My God how the money rolls in.

My aunt keeps a girls' seminary,
Teaching young girls to begin,
She doesn't say where they finish,
My God how the money rolls in.

I've lost all me cash on the horses,
I'm sick from the illicit gin,
I'm falling in love with my father,
My God what a mess I am in.

Oh, dear, what can the matter be,
Seven old ladies locked in the lavatory,
They were there from Sunday to Saturday,
Nobody knew they were there.

They said they were going to
have tea with the Vicar,
They went in together,
they thought it was quicker,
But the lavatory door was a bit of a sticker,
And the Vicar had tea all alone.

The first was the wife of a deacon in Dover,
And though she was known
as a bit of a rover,
She liked it so much
she thought she'd stay over,
And nobody knew she was there.

The next old lady was old Mrs Bickle,
She found herself in a desperate pickle,
Shut in a pay booth, she hadn't a nickel,
And nobody knew she was there.

The next was the
Bishop of Chichester's daughter,
Who went in to pass some superfluous water,
She pulled on the chain
and the rising tide caught her,
And nobody knew she was there.

The next old lady with Abigail Humphrey,
Who settled inside to make herself comfy,
And then she found out
she could not get her bum free
And nobody knew she was there.

The next old lady was Elizabeth Spender,
Who was doing all right
till a vagrant suspender
Got all twisted up in her feminine gender,
And nobody knew she was there.

The last was a lady named Jennifer Trim,
She only sat down on a personal whim
But she somehow got pinched
twixt the cup and the brim,
And nobody knew she was there.

But another old lady was Mrs McBligh,
Went in with a bottle to booze on the sly,
She jumped on the seat
and fell in with a cry,
And nobody knew she was there.

IF I WERE THE MARRYING KIND

If I were the marrying kind,
Which thank the Lord I'm not, sir,
The kind of man that I would wed
Would be a rugby full-back.

And he'd find touch and I'd find touch,
We'd both touch together,
We'd be all right in the middle of the night
Finding touch together.

If I were the marrying kind,
Which thank the Lord I'm not, sir,
The kind of man that I would wed
Would be a wing three-quarter.

And he'd go hard and I'd go hard,
We'd both go hard together,
We'd be all right in the middle of the night
Going hard together.

If I were the marrying kind,
Which thank the Lord I'm not, sir,
The kind of man that I would wed
Would be a centre three-quarter.

And he'd pass it out and I'd pass it out,
We'd both pass it out together,
We'd be all right in the middle of the night
Passing it out together.

If I were the marrying kind,
Which thank the Lord I'm not, sir,
The kind of man that I would wed
Would be a rugby fly-half.

And he'd whip it out and I'd whip it out,
We'd both whip it out together,
We'd be all right in the middle of the night
Whipping it out together.

If I were the marrying kind,
Which thank the Lord I'm not, sir,
The kind of man that I would wed
Would be a rugby scrum-half.

And he'd put it in and I'd put it in,
We'd both put it in together,
We'd be all right in the middle of the night
Putting it in together.

If I were the marrying kind,
Which thank the Lord I'm not, sir,
The kind of man that I would wed
Would be a rugby hooker.

And he'd strike hard and I'd strike hard,
We'd both strike hard together,
We'd be all right in the middle of the night
Striking hard together.

If I were the marrying kind,
Which thank the Lord I'm not, sir,
The kind of man that I would wed
Would be a big prop-forward.

And he'd bind tight and I'd bind tight,
We'd both bind tight together,
We'd be all right in the middle of the night
Binding tight together.

If I were the marrying kind,
Which thank the Lord I'm not, sir,
The kind of man that I would wed
Would be a referee.

And he would blow and I would blow
We'd both blow together,
We'd be all right in the middle of the night
Blowing hard together.

ROLL ME OVER IN THE CLOVER

This is number one
and the fun has just begun,
Roll me over, lay me down and do it again,
Roll me over in the clover,
Roll me over, lay me down and do it again.

Oh, this is number two
and my hand is on her shoe.
Oh, this is number three
and my hand is on her knee.
Oh, this is number four
and we're rolling on the floor.
Oh, this is number five
and the bee is in the hive.
Oh, this is number six
and she said she liked my tricks.
Oh, this is number seven
and we're in our seventh heaven.
Oh, this is number eight
and the nurse is at the gate.
Oh, this is number nine
and the twins are doing fine.
Oh, this is number ten
and we're at it once again.
Oh, this is number eleven
and we start again from seven.
Oh, this is number twelve
and she said: "Nu kan jag sjalv."

Oh, this is number twenty
and she said that that was plenty.
Oh, this is number thirty
and she said that was dirty.
Oh, this is number forty
and she said: "Now you are naughty."

RIP MY KNICKERS AWAY

Be I Berkshire, be I buggery,
Oi koms up from Wareham,
Oi knows a gal with calico drawers,
And I knows how to tear 'em.

Chorus: Rip my knickers away,
rip my knickers away,
I don't care what becomes of me,
As long as you finger my
       *__*__*__*.
Rip my knickers away, away,
Rip my knickers away,
Down the front, down the back,
Round the ****, round the crack,
Rip my knickers away.

Walkin' by the field one day
I heard a maiden crying,
"Oh, please don't rip me knickers off, Jack,
You'll get there by and byin'."

THE RAJAH OF ASTRAKHAN

There was a Rajah of Astrakhan,
A most licentious lout of a man,
Of wives he had a hundred and nine,
Including his favourite concubine.

One day when there was no one at hand
He called to a warrior, one of his band,
"Go down to my harem, you lazy swine,
And fetch my favourite concubine."

The warrior fetched the concubine,
A figure like Venus, a face divine,
The Rajah give a significant grunt
And placed himself within her arms.

The Rajah bellowed loud and long,
The maiden answered sure and strong,
But just when all had come to a head,
They both fell through the rickety bed.

They hit the floor with a hell of a crack,
Which completely ruined the poor girl's back,
And as for the Rajah's magnificent end,
It split down the middle and started to bend.

There is a moral to this tale,
There is a moral to this tale,
If you would try a girl at all
Stick her right up against the wall.

Oh, she was a cripple with only one nipple
To feed the baby on.
Poor little ******, he'd only one sucker
To start his life upon.

    Twenty-one, never been done,
    Queen of all the fairies.

Ain't it a pity she'd only one titty
To feed the baby on.
Poor little bugger, he'll never play rugger,
Nor grow up big and strong.

    Twenty-one, never been done,
    Queen of all the fairies.

And as he got older and bolder and bolder,
And took himself in hand,
And flipped and flipped
and flipped and flipped,
To the tune of an army band.
They tried him in the infantry,
They tried him on the land and sea,
The poor little bugger had no success,
He left everything in a terrible mess,
We see no hope for him unless
He joins the W.R.A.F.

    Twenty-one, never been done,
    Queen of all the fairies.

PUT ON YOUR BUSTLE

Put on your old bustle
And get out and hustle
For tomorrow the rent man is due.
Put your **** in clover
With another loaded lover
And don't return without a quid or two.

Put on your old pink panties
The ones that were your aunty's
Let's have a shageroo in the hay,
And while they're working in the field
We'll see what the crop can yield,
In that good old fashioned way.

Put on your old suspenders
And get to mixing up the genders,
There isn't any risk anyway,
For the stud's been altered,
And the bull's been haltered
In that good old fashioned way.

Put on your old grey corset,
If it don't fit force it,
For the army is moving in today,
As the bee makes honey
Let your **** make money
In the good old fashioned way.

Put on the old green ointment
The fleas disappointment,

And kill the buggers where they lay,
How it tickles and itches,
It'll kill the sons of bitches
In that good old fashioned way.

I went with Mabel to a surgeon,
For to see what he could do,
Said the surgeon, "She's no virgin,
Sixty quid or no can do."

Ribald creatures are the crayfish,
When a litter they essay,
Yes, my hearties, they give parties,
In the good old fashioned way.

Please to think of the careful codfish,
Always when the missus calls,
A female codfish is an odd fish,
She too gives us codfish balls.

The trout is just a tiny salmon,
Hardly grown it has no scales,
Yet the trout, just like the salmon,
Can't get on without his tails.

Shad roe comes from a harlot shad fish,
Shad fish faced a sorry fate,
A pregnant shad fish is a sad fish,
She gets that way without a mate.

The old mockturtle's mate is happy,
O'er her lover's charming ways,
First he grips her with his flipper
Then he flips for days and days.

Caviar comes from the virgin sturgeon,
The virgin sturgeon's a very fine fish,
The virgin sturgeon needs no urgin'
That's why caviar is my dish.

Chorus: My ruddy oath it is,
my ruddy oath it is.

I gave caviar to my girl friend,
She was a virgin tried and true,
Ever since she had that caviar,
There ain't nothing she won't do.

I gave caviar to my grandpa,
Grandpa's age is ninety-three,
And next time I saw grandpa,
He'd chased grandma up a tree.

My father was a lighthouse keeper,
He had caviar for his tea,
He had three children by a mermaid,
Two were kippers, one was me.

I gave caviar to my bow-wow,
All the others looked agog,
He had what those bitches wanted,
Wasn't he a lucky dog?

Oysters are prolific bivalves,
Rear their young ones in their shell,
How they piddle is a riddle,
But they do, so what the hell.

The female clam is optimistic,
Shoots her eggs out in the sea,
She hopes her suitor as a shooter,
Hits the self-same spot as she.

Phyllis Quat she died in the springtime,
She expired in a terrible fit,
We fulfilled her last dying wish, sir,
She was buried in six feet of —

Chorus: Sweet violets,
sweeter than all the roses,
Covered all over from **** to ***
Covered all over with ****.

Phyllis Quat kept a sack in the garden
I was curious I must admit,
One day I stuck in my finger
And pulled it out covered in —

Phyllis Quat took a bag to her boy friend's
But the bag was old and it split,
Now the boy friend
and Phyllis have parted
For the bag was packed quite full of —

I sat on a gold lavatory
In the home of the Baron of Split,
The seat was encrusted with rubies
But as usual the bowl contained —

There was a professional farter
Who could flatulate ballads and airs,
He could poop out the Moonlight Sonata
And accompany musical chairs, singing —

One day he attempted an opera
It was hard but the fool wouldn't quit,
With his head held aloft
he suddenly coughed
And collapsed in a big heap of ****.

Well, now my song it is ended
And I have finished my bit
And if any of you feel offended
Stick your head in a bucket of ****.

This is the tale of Sonia Snell
To whom an accident befell,
An accident, as will be seen,
Embarrassing in the extreme.
It happened as it does to many
That Sonia went to spend a penny,
And entering with unconscious grace
The properly appointed place,
There behind the railway station
She sat in silent meditation,
Unfortunately unacquainted
The seat had recently been painted.
Too late did Sonia realize
Her inability to rise,
And though she struggled, pulled and yelled
She found that she was firmly held.
She raised her voice in mournful shout,
"Please, someone, come and get me out."
A crowd stood round and feebly sniggered,
A signalman said: "I'll be jiggered."
"Gor blimey," said an ancient porter,
"We ought to soak her orf wiv water."
The station master and his staff
Were most polite and did not laugh.
They tugged at Sonia's hands and feet
But could not shift her off the seat.
A carpenter arrived at last
And finding Sonia still stuck fast

Remarked: "I know what I can do."
And quickly sawed the seat in two.
Sonia arose, only to find
She'd a wooden halo on her behind,
But an ambulance drove down the street
And bore her off complete with seat.
They rushed the wood-bustled girl
Quickly into hospital
And grasping her hands and head
Placed her face downwards on a bed.
The doctors came and cast their eyes
Upon the seat with some surprise.
A surgeon said: "Now mark my word
Could anything be more absurd?
Have any of you, I implore,
Seen anything like this before?"
"Yes," cried a student, unashamed,
"Frequently—but never framed."

SMALL BOYS

Small boys are cheap today
Cheaper than yesterday.
Small ones are half a crown,
Standing up or lying down.
Big ones are four and six
'Cause they've got bigger dicks,
Small boys are cheap, cheaper today.

THE SEXUAL LIFE OF THE CAMEL

The sexual life of the camel
Is stranger than anyone thinks,
At the height of the mating season
He tries to bugger the sphinx,
But the sphinx's posterior sphincter
Is all clogged by the sands of the Nile,
Which accounts for the hump on the camel
And the sphinx's inscrutable smile.

In the process of syphilization
From the anthropoid ape down to man
It is generally held that the Navy
Has buggered whatever it can,
Yet recent extensive researches
By Darwin and Huxley and Hall
Conclusively prove that the hedgehog
Has never been buggered at all.

We therefore believe our conclusion
Is incontrovertibly shown
That comparative safety on shipboard
Is enjoyed by the hedgehog alone.
Why haven't they done it at Spithead,
As they've done it at Harvard and Yale
And also at Oxford and Cambridge
By shaving the spines off its tail.

THE ONE-EYED RILEY

Sitting in O'Riley's bar one day
Telling yarns of blood and slaughter
Suddenly a thought came into my head
Why not **** O'Riley's daughter?

Chorus: Yippee-I-aye, yippee-I-aye,
         Yippee-I-aye for the one-eyed Riley
         *********, rissoles,
         ***** and all
         Shove it up the nearest ****.

I took the fair girl by the hand
Gently swung my left leg over,
Never a word the sweet child said
Laughed like hell till the fun was over.

I heard a footstep on the stair
Who could it be but the one-eyed Riley
With two pistols in his hands,
Looking for the man
who had ****** his daughter.

I grabbed O'Riley by the hair,
Shoved his hair in a tub o' water
Stuffed his pistols up his ****
Bloody sight quicker
than I stuffed his daughter!

WILL YOU MARRY ME?

If I give you half-a-crown
Can I take your knickers down,
Will you marry, marry marry marry, marry,
Will you marry me?

If you give me half-a-crown
You can't take my knickers down,
You can't marry, marry marry marry, marry,
You can't marry me.

If I give you fish and chips
*Will you let me squeeze your ****,*
Will you marry, marry marry marry, marry,
Will you marry me?

If you give me fish and chips
*I won't let you squeeze my ****,*
You can't marry, marry marry marry, marry,
You can't marry me.

If I give you my big chest
And all the money I possess,
Will you marry, marry marry marry, marry,
Will you marry me?

If you give me your big chest
And all the money you possess,
I will marry, marry marry marry, marry,
I will marry you.

Get out of the door, you lousy whore,
My money was all you were looking for,
And I'll not marry, marry marry
marry, marry,
I'll not marry you.

FLY AWAY YOU BUMBLE BEE

Sambo was a lazy coon
Who used to sleep in the afternoon
    So tired was he
    So tired was he
Off to the forest he would go
Swinging his hands to and fro
    When along came a bee
    A bloody great bumble bee
    Bzz, bzz, bzz, bzz

"Get away you bumble bee
I ain't no rose
I ain't no syphilitic bastard
*Get off my ******* nose.*
Get off my nasal organ
Don't you come near
If you wants bit o' fanny
*You can **** my granny*
*But you'll get no ****hole here.*

    *****hole rules the Navy*
    *****hole rules the sea*
    If you wants bit o' bum
    *You can **** my chum*
    *But you'll get no **** from me!*

THE BALLS OF O'LEARY

The ***** of O'Leary
are massive and hairy
They're shapely and stately
like the dome of St Paul's
People all muster to view the great cluster
They stand and they stare
at the bloody great pair
Of O'Leary's *****.

THE ENGINEER'S DREAM

An engineer told me before he died
And I've no reason to believe he lied
He knew a woman with a **** so wide
That she was never satisfied.

So he built a ***** of steel
Driven by a bloody great wheel
Two brass balls he filled with cream
And the whole bloody
issue was driven by steam.

Round and round
went the bloody great wheel
In and out went the ***** of steel
'Till at last the maiden cried,
"Enough, enough, I'm satisfied."

Up and up went the level of steam
Down and down went the level of cream,
'Till again the maiden cried,
"Enough, enough, I'm satisfied."

Now we come to the tragic bit
There was no way of stopping it
She was split from **** to tit.
And the whole bloody issue was covered in
****.

THE TATTOOED LADY

One night in gay Paree
I paid five francs to see
A much tattooed lady
A big fat French lady
Tattooed from head to knee
And on her jaw
Was a British man-o-war
And in the middle of her back
Was a Union Jack
So I paid three francs more
And up and down her spine
Were the old die-hards in line
And on her big fat bum
Was a picture of the rising sun
And on her fanny
Was Al Johnson singing "Mammy"
How I loves her, How I loves her
My mother in law.

I loves my mother in law
She is nothing but a dirty old whore
She nags me day and night
*I can't do **** all right*
Last night I heard
she was coming round to stay
Now isn't it a pity
She only has one titty
And in the family way.

Last night I greased the stairs
Put tin-tacks on the chairs
I hope she breaks her back
Because I do love wearing black
Now Tommy Tucker
*Is a stupid little ******
How I loves her, how I loves her,
How I loves my mother-in-law.

Chorus: *Young folk, old folk*
   Everybody come
   To the darkie Sunday School
   And we'll have lots of fun
   Bring your sticks of chewing gum
   And sit upon the floor
   And we'll tell you Bible stories
   That you've never heard before.

Now Adam was the first man
So we're led to believe
He walked into the garden
And bumped right into Eve
There was no one there to show him
But he quickly found the way
And that's the very reason
Why we're singing here today.

The Lord said unto Noah
"It's going to rain today"
So Noah built a bloody great Ark
In which to sail away,
The animals went in two by two
But soon got up to tricks
So, although they came in two by two
They came out six by six.

Now Moses in the bullrushes
Was all wrapped up in swathe

Pharaoh's daughter found him
When she went down there to bathe
She took him back to Pharaoh
And said, "I found him on the shore"
And Pharaoh winked his eye and said
"I've heard that one before."

King Solomon and King David
Lived most immoral lives
Spent their time a-chasing
After other people's wives
The Lord spake unto both of them
And it worked just like a charm
'Cos Solomon wrote the Proverbs
And David wrote the Psalms.

Now Samson was an Israelite
And very big and strong
Delilah was a Philistine
Always doing wrong.
They spent a week together
But it didn't get very hot
For all he got was a short back and sides
And a little bit off the top.

MONTE CARLO

As she walked along the Bois de Boulogne
With a heart as heavy as lead
She wishes that she was dead
She had lost her maidenhead
Her heart in a funk and covered with *****
Her knickers were torn
and her **** *was worn*
She's the girl that lowered the price
at Monte Carlo.

As he walked along the Bois de Boulogne
With his ***** *upon the stand*
The girls all say it's grand
To take it in their hand
You give them a bob and they're on the job
Pulling the foreskin over the knob
Of the man who broke the bank
at Monte Carlo.

CHRISTOPHER ROBIN

Little boy kneels at the foot of the stairs
Clutched in his hand
are a bunch of white hairs
Oh my just fancy that
Christopher Robin castrated the cat.

Little boy kneels at the foot of the bed
Lily-white hands are caressing his head
Oh my could'nt be worse
Christopher Robin is shagging his nurse.

Little boy sits on the lavatory pan
Gently caressing his little old man
Flip flop into the tank
Christopher Robin is having a wank.

Miss Jones was walking down the street,
When a young fella she happened to meet
Who was giving the girls a helluva treat
By twisting and turning his *****.

Chorus: For they were large *****, large
*   *****,*
*   Twice as heavy as lead*
*   With a dexterous twist*
*   of his muscular wrist*
*   He threw them right over his head.*

A policeman to the scene was brought
He said, "I'll have to take you to court
'Cos it's certain that nobody ought
To be twisting and turning his *****."

The prisoner standing in the dock
Gave the judge a helluva shock
By insisting on showing the jury his ****
And twisting and turning his *****.

The judge he said, "The case is clear
The fine will be a barrel of beer
For any young bugger who comes in here
Twisting and turning his *****."

IN THE SHADE OF THE OLD APPLE TREE

In the shade of the old apple tree
A pair of fine legs I did see
With some hair at the top
And a little red spot
It looked like a cherry to me.

I pulled out my pride of New York
It fitted it just like a cork
I said, "Darlin' don't scream
While I fill you with cream
In the shade of the old apple tree."

And as we both lay on the grass
With my two hands around her fat ****
She said, "If you'll be true
You can have a **** too!
In the shade of the old apple tree."

THE RAM OF DERBYSHIRE

There was a ram of Derbyshire
That had two horns of brass,
The one grew out of its head, sir,
*The other grew out of its ****.*

Chorus: If you don't believe me
Or if you think I lie
Go ask the girls of Derbyshire
They'll tell you the same as I.

When the ram was young, sir,
It had a nasty trick
Of jumping over a five-barred gate
*And landing on its *****.*

When the ram was old, sir,
They put in a truck
And all the girls of Derbyshire
*Came out to have a ****.*

When the ram was dead, sir,
They buried it in St Paul's,
It took twelve men and a donkey cart
*To carry away its *****.*

THE HOLE IN THE ELEPHANT'S BOTTOM

My ambition's to go on the stage;
From this you can see that I've got 'em.
In pantomime I'm all the rage,
I'm the hole in the elephant's bottom.

Oh! The girls think that I'm it,
As they sit in the stalls I can spot 'em,
And I wink at the girls in the pit
Through the hole in the elephant's bottom.

One night we performed in a farce
And they stuffed up the bottom with cotton,
*But it split and I showed my bare ****
Through the hole in the elephant's bottom.

There are pockets inside in the cloth
For two bottles of Bass, if you've got 'em.
But they hiss and they boo
when I blow out the froth
Through the hole in the elephant's bottom.

Now my part hasn't got any words
But there's nothing that can't be forgotten,
*I spend all my time pushing property *****
Through the hole in the elephant's bottom.

Some may think that this story is good
And some may believe that it's rotten,
But those that don't like it
can stuff it right up
The hole in the elephant's bottom.

Should the Japanese make an attack,
Then hundreds of bombs—
they will drop 'em,
But we'll keep 'em at bay
with an Oerliken gun
Through the hole in the elephant's bottom.

SOME DIE OF DRINKING WATER

Some die of drinking water
And some of drinking beer
Some die of constipation
And some of diarrhoea
But of all the world's diseases
There's none that can compare
With the drip, drip, drip
of a syphilitic *****
And they call it gonorrhoea.

I like the girls who say they will
I like the girls who won't
I hate the girls who say they will
And then they say they won't
But of all the girls I like the best
I may be wrong or right
Are the girls who say they never will
But look as though they might.

On Sunday afternoon
While the church was turning out
The Vicar said to me,
"I bet I've been through
More women than you."
And the verger said, "You're on.
We'll stand by the gate
While the women pass by
And this shall be our sign
You ding dong for the women you've had
And I'll ping pong for mine."

There were ding dongs
There were ping pongs
There were more ding dongs
Than there were ping pongs
Till at last a woman went by
And the curate said, "Ding dong"
"Just a minute," said the Vicar,
"There's a mistake here
That is my wife I do declare."
"I don't give a bugger
I've still been there
Ding a dong, ding a dong, ding a dong,
Ding Dong."

CAROLINA

Way down in Alabama
where the bull-****lies thick
The girls are so pretty
that the babies come quick
There lives Carolina the queen of them all
Carolina, Carolina the cow-puncher's whore.

She's handy, she's bandy,
she shags in the street
Whenever you meet her she's always on heat
If you leave your flies open,
she's after your meat
And the smell of her ****
knocks you right off your feet.

One night I was riding
way down by the falls
One hand on my pistol, the other on my balls
I saw Carolina using a stick
Instead of the end of a cow-puncher's *****.

I caressed her, undressed her
and laid her down there
And parted the tresses of curly-brown hair
Inserted the ***** of my sturdy horse
And then there began a strange intercourse.

157

Faster and faster went my sturdy steed
Until Carolina rejoiced at the speed
When all of a sudden my horse did back-fire
And shot Carolina right into the mire.

Up got Carolina all covered in muck,
*And said, "Oh dear, what a glorious ****."*
Two paces forward and fell flat on the floor
And that was the end
of the cow-puncher's whore.

BOY MEETS GIRL

Boy meets girl, holds her hand,
Visions of a promised land,
Tender words, cling and kiss,
Crafty feel, heavenly bliss,
Nibble nipples, squeeze thighs,
Gets a beat, feels a rise,
Eyes ablaze, drawers down,
Really starts to go to town,
Legs outspread, virgin lass,
Fanny foams like bottled Bass,
Ram it home, moans of joy,
Teenage love, girl meets boy,
Love's a jewel, pearls he's won,
Shoots his load, what's he done,
Comes the pay off, here's the rub,
He's got her in the pudding club,
Comes the wedding, bridesmaids flap,
Love and cherish, all that crap,
A tubby tum, weighty gain,
Prams and nappies, labour pain,
Begins to realise what he did,
Nagging wife and screaming kid,
*Sweats his ***** off, works his stint;*
Only pleasure is evening time,
When mattress creaks she's off again,
Can't forsake those sexy habits,
Breeding kids like bloody rabbits.

YOUR SPOONING DAYS

Your spooning days are over,
Your pilot light is out,
What used to be your sex appeal
Is now your water spout.

You used to be embarrassed
To make the thing behave,
For every blooming morning
It would stand up and watch you shave.

But now you are growing old,
It sure gives you the blues,
To see the thing hang down your leg,
And watch you shine your shoes.

*Chorus: That was a jolly old song
        Sing us another one do.*

*There was a young lady named Hilda
Who went for a walk with a builder
He knew that he could
And he should, and he would—
And he did—and he goddam near killed
her!*

*The jolly old Bishop of Birmingham
He buggered three maids while confirming
'em.
As they knelt seeking God
He excited his rod
And pumped his episcopal sperm in 'em.*

*There was a young couple named Kelly
Who were found stuck belly to belly,
Because in their haste
They used library paste
Instead of petroleum jelly.*

*There was a young lady of Cheam
Who crept into the vestry unseen
She pulled down her knickers
Likewise the vicar's
And said, "How about it, old bean?"*

A chap down in Oklahoma
Had a **** that could sing La Paloma,
But the sweetness of pitch
Couldn't put off the hitch
Of impotence, size and aroma.

There was a young fellow from Leeds
Who swallowed a package of seeds.
Great tufts of grass
Sprouted out of his ****
And his ***** were all covered with weeds.

There was a young girl of Detroit
Who at ******* was very adroit
She could squeeze her vagina
To a pin-point, or finer
Or open it out like a quoit.

A disgusting young man named McGill
Made his neighbours exceedingly ill
When they learned of his habits
Involving white rabbits
And a bird with a flexible bill.

There was a young man of St Johns
Who wanted to bugger the swans.
"Oh no," said the porter,
"You bugger my daughter,
Them swans is reserved for the Dons."

A handsome young monk in a wood
Told a girl she should cling to the good.

She obeyed him, and gladly;
He repulsed her, but sadly,
"My dear, you have misunderstood."

There was a young maid from Mobile
Whose **** was made of blue steel.
She got her thrills
From pneumatic drills
And off-centred emery wheels.

There was a young lady of Crewe
Whose cherry a chap had got through
Which she told to her mother
Who fixed her another
Out of rubber and red ink and glue.

When a lecherous cunrate at Leeds
Was discovered, one day, in the weeds
Astride a young nun,
He said, "Christ this is fun,
Far better than telling one's beads!"

There was a young man from Cape Cod
Who put his own mother in pod.
His name? It was Tucker,
The Bugger, The ******,
The Bleeder, The Bastard, The Sod.

There was a young girl of Dundee
Who was raped by an ape in a tree.
The result was most horrid—
All **** and no forehead,
Three **** and a purple goatee.

There was a young lady of Twickenham,
Who regretted that men had no *****in 'em.
On her knees every day,
To her God she would pray
To lengthen, and strengthen,
and thicken 'em.

There was a young girl named McCall
Whose **** was exceedingly small,
But the size of her anus
Was something quite heinous—
It could hold seven ****** and one ****.

There was a young man from Lynn
Whose **** was the size of a pin.
Said his girl with a laugh
As she fondled his staff,
"This won't be much of a sin."

A broken down harlot named Tupps
Was heard to confess in her cups:
"The height of my folly
Was ******* a collie—
But I got a nice price for the pups."

There was a young man of high station
Who was found by a pious relation
Making love in a ditch
To—I won't say a bitch—
But a woman of no reputation.

There was a young German named Ringer
Who was screwing an opera singer.

Said he with a grin,
"Well, I've sure got it in!"
Said she, "You mean that ain't your finger?"

A young man with passions quite gingery
Tore a hole in his sister's best lingerie.
He slapped her behind
And made up his mind
To add incest to insult and injury.

There was a young man of Belgravia,
Who cared neither for God nor his Saviour,
He walked down the Strand
With his ***** in his hand,
And was had up for indecent behaviour.

There was a young nun from Siberia
Endowed with a virgin interior—
Until an old monk
Jumped into her bunk
And now she's the Mother Superior.

There was a young Scot from Delray
Who buggered his father one day,
Saying, "I like it rather
To stuff it up Father
He's clean and there's nothing to pay."

There was a young plumber of Lea
Who was plumbing a girl by the sea.
She said, "Stop your plumbing;
There's somebody coming!"
Said the plumber, still plumbing, "It's me."

There was an old man of Dundee,
Who came home as drunk as could be.
He wound up the clock
With the end of his ****
And buggered his wife with the key.

There was a young parson named Binns
Who talked about women and things.
But his secret desire
Was a boy in the choir
With a bottom like jelly on springs.

An elderly pervert in Nice
Who was long past wanting a piece
Would jack-off his hogs
His cows and his dogs,
Till his parrot called in the police.

All the lady-apes ran from King Kong
For his dong was unspeakably long.
But a friendly giraffe
Quaffed his yard and a half
And ecstatically burst into song.

A maiden who lived in Virginny
Had a **** that could bark,
neigh and whinny.
The hunting set chased her,
******, buggered, then dropped her
For the pitch of her organ went tinny.

There was a young girl of Devon
Who was raped in the garden by seven
High Anglican Priests—
The lascivious beasts—
Of such is the kingdom of Heaven.

When a woman in strapless attire
Found her breasts
working higher and higher,
A guest, with great feeling,
Exclaimed, "How appealing!
Do you mind if I piss in the fire?"

There was a young lady of Trent
Who said that she knew what it meant
When he asked her to dine,
Private room, lots of wine
She knew, oh she knew—but she went!

There was a young lady named Hitchin
Who was scratching
her crotch in the kitchen.
Her mother, said, "Rose,
It's the crabs, I suppose."
She said, "Yes, and the buggers are itchin'."

There was a young man of St James
Who indulged in the jolliest games:
He lighted the rim
Of his grandmother's ****,
And laughed as she pissed
through the flames.

A fellow whose surname was Hunt
Trained his **** to perform a slick stunt:
This versatile spout
Could be turned inside out
Like a glove, and be used as a ****.

There was a young lady from Kew
Who filled her vagina with glue.
She said with a grin,
"If they pay to get in,
They'll pay to get out of it too."

An organist playing in York
Had a ***** that could hold a small fork,
And between obbligatos
He'd munch at tomatoes
And keep up his strength while at work.

There was a young girl of Darjeeling
Who could dance with such exquisite feeling
There was never a sound
For miles around
Save of fly-buttons hitting the ceiling.

A lady while dining at Crewe
Found an elephant's dong in her stew.
Said the waiter, "Don't shout,
And don't wave it about,
Or the others will all want one too."

A hermit who had an oasis
Thought it the best of all places;

He could pray and be calm
'Neath a pleasant date-palm
While the lice on his ******** ran races.

There was a young fellow named Kimble
Whose ***** was exceedingly nimble,
But fragile and slender,
And dainty and tender
So he kept it encased in a thimble.

The last time I dined with the King
He did quite a curious thing:
He sat on a stool
And took out his ****
And said, "If I play, will you sing?"

The gay young Duke of Buckingham
Stood on the bridge at Rockingham
Watching the stunts
Of the ***** and the punts
And the tricks of the ****** that were
    ******* 'em.

A mathematician named Hall
Had a hexahedronical ball,
And the cube of its weight
Times his pecker, plus eight,
Was four-fifths of five-eighths ****-all.

There was a young student of Trinity
Who shattered his sister's virginity
He buggered his brother

Had twins by his mother
And took double honour in Divinity.

There was a young fellow named Scott
Who took a girl out on his yacht—
But too lazy to rape her
He made darts of brown paper
Which he languidly tossed at her ****.

There was a young lady of Exeter,
So pretty, that men craned their necks at her.
One went so far
As to wave from his car
The distinguishing mark of his sex at her.

Rosalina, a pretty young lass,
Had a truly magnificent ass:
Not rounded and pink
As you possibly think—
It was grey, had long ears, and ate grass.

WHY WAS HE BORN SO BEAUTIFUL

Why was he born so beautiful?
Why was he born at all?
*He's no ******* use to anyone*
*He's no ******* use at all.*

BE KIND TO YOUR WEB-FOOTED FRIENDS

Be kind to your web-footed friends
For a duck may be somebody's mother
Be kind to your friends in the swamp
Where the weather is cool and damp
Now you may think that this is the end
Well it is . . .

WHOREDEAN SCHOOL

We are from Whoredean—
Whoredean girls are we,
We take no pride in our virginity,
We take precautions
And avoid abortions
For we are from Whoredean School.

*Chorus: Up school, up school, **** the*
school,
La, la, la, la, la la la la la, hoi.

Our house mistress you cannot beat,
She lets us go walking in the street.
We sell our titties for threepenny bitties
Right outside Whoredean School.

Our school doctor, she is a beaut,
Teaches us to swerve
when our boy friends shoot,
It saves many marriages
And forced miscarriages,
For we are from Whoredean School.

Our head prefect, her name is Jane,
She only likes it now and again,
And again and again,
And again and again,
And again and again and again.

We go to Whoredean, don't we have pluck
We go to bed without asking a buck,
Try us sometime boys
You may be in luck
For we are from Whoredean School.

Our sports mistress she is the best,
Teaches us to develop our chest,
So we wear tight sweaters,
And carry French letters,
For we are from Whoredean School.

We are at Whoredean each Whitsun dance,
We don't wear bras
and we don't wear pants,
We like to give our boy friends a chance,
For we are from Whoredean School.

Our school porter he is a fool,
He's only got a teeny weeny ****,
It's all right for key holes
And little girl's peeholes,
But not much good for Whoredean School.

Our school gardener he makes us drool,
He's got a great big whopping, dirty ****,
All right for tunnels
and Queen Mary funnels,
And for the girls of Whoredean School.

We go to Whoredean, don't we have fun,
We know exactly how it is done,
When we lie down we hole it in one,
For we are from Whoredean School.

We have a new girl, her name is Flo,
Nobody thought that she could have a go,
But she surprised the Vicar
By raising him quicker
Than any other girl at Whoredean School.

These girls from Cheltenham,
They are just sissies,
They get worked up over one or two kisses,
It takes wax candles,
And long broom handles,
To rouse the bowels
of girls from Whoredean School.

We go to Whoredean, we can be had,
Don't take our word, boy,
ask your old Dad,
He brings his friends
for breath-taking trends,
For we are from Whoredean School.

When we go down to the sea for a swim,
The people remark on the size of our ****,
You can bet your bottom dollar,
It's big as a horse's collar,
For we are from Whoredean School.

WORKING DOWN THE SEWER

Chorus: Workin' down the sewer
shovellin' up manure,
That's the way the soldier
*does his bit, shovelling ****.*
You can hear the shovels ring
with a ting-a-ling-a-ling,
When you're working down
the sewer with the gang.

Now the foreman said to me,
*As he grabbed me by the ****,*
"You're the dirtiest little bastard
That we have upon the job.
Your wages for the week
Will be five and twenty bob,
When you're working down
the sewer with the gang."

One morning after eight,
When I turned up at the gate,
The foreman said to me,
*"Now ******* look 'ere mate,*
*If you won't come ******* early*
*Then you can't come ******* late,*
When you're workin' down
the sewer with the gang."

WHEN LADY JANE BECAME A TART

It fairly broke the family's heart
When Lady Jane became a tart
But blood is blood and race is race
And so to save the family face
They bought her an expensive flat
With "Welcome" written on the mat.

It was not long ere Lady Jane
Brought her patrician charms to fame
A clientele of sahibs pukka
Who regularly came to **** 'er,
And it was whispered without malice
She had a client from the palace.

No one could nestle in her charms
Unless he wore ancestral arms
No one to her could gain an entry,
Unless he were of the landed gentry,
And so before her sun had set
She'd worked her way through Debrett.

When Lady Anne became a whore
It grieved the family even more,
But they felt they couldn't do the same
As they had done for Lady Jane,
So they bought her an exclusive beat,
On the shady side of Jermyn Street.

When Lord St Clancy became a nancy
It did not please the family fancy
And so in order to protect him
They did inscribe upon his rectum,
"All commoners must now drive steerage,
*This ****hole is reserved for peerage."*

I'm a bachelor's son and I live in sin
With another man's wife at The Cross,
I've a fantan pool, a two-up school,
a brothel and a fourpenny doss.

Chorus: And when I die I'll surely fry
In the brimstone pots of hell,
But until that day,
and if you can pay,
Then I have sin to sell.

I've three ex-wives running sly grog dives,
And my brother forges ten-pound notes,
For a union on the rocks
we can rig a ballot box,
With a million phoney votes.

I sell sex to moral wrecks
And drugs to damn your nerves,
Abortions, too, I can fix for you,
We've a special line for perves.

Lesbian love and incest, too,
And flagellists quite a few,
And I've a special file
marked "Utterly Vile"
And an embalmed corpse
for a homonecrophile.

MISS MILLY

Young Miss Milly was sweet and fair,
With snow white **** and curly hair,
Oh, unhappy maiden.
Her heart was happy, her step was light,
But she was a fool and one dark night
She got herself put in a pregnant plight
By a lecherous, lewd and
lustful cruel deceiver.

She went to his home but as she'd feared
The filthy old ****** had disappeared,
Oh, unhappy maiden.
Her mother declared: "Get out, you whore.
No daughter of mine breaks chastity's law,
So never again dare to darken my door,
With your lecherous, lewd and
lustful cruel deceiver."

All night she wandered through the snow
How she suffered who can know,
Oh, unhappy maiden.
And when the morning cockerel cried,
Poor abandoned Milly had died
Frozen stiff as she lay outside.
Oh, the lecherous, lewd and
lustful cruel deceiver.

Hark all you young maidens,
the moral is clear
If you trust these foul bastards,
you'll shed many a tear
Like this oh, so unhappy maiden.
So bear this in mind: the semen may spill
And you'll find yourself getting
more than your fill.
Precautions are best;
take a birth control pill.
With your lecherous, lewd and
lustful cruel deceiver.

We wanna sail but we're out of luck,
The skipper's dead drunk
in the Dog and Duck.

Chorus: Stormy weather, boys,
stormy weather, boys,
When the wind blows
the barge will go.

Skipper come aboard with a girl on his arm,
Come along me pretty missy,
there's no cause for alarm.

He said he liked her very, very much,
He asked her if she'd shag
and she kicked him in the crutch,

Skipper's dead drunk
in the Dog and the Duck
Asking the barmaid if he can have a ****.

Cook said he shouldn't be a skipper
on a punt
We're all agreed he's a silly old ****.

If all the whores with dirty drawers
Were lying in the Strand
Do you suppose, the Walrus said
That we could raise a stand?
I doubt it, said the Carpenter
But wouldn't it be grand
And all the while the dirty sod
Was coming in his hand.

When you were only sweet sixteen
And had a little quim
You stood before the looking-glass
And put one finger in
But now that you are old and grey
And losing all your charm
I can get five fingers in
*And half my ******* arm.*

She went for a drive in a Morgan,
She sat with the driver in front.
He fooled with her genital organs:
*The more vulgar-minded say "****".*

Now she had a figure ethereal,
*She auctioned it out to men's *****,*
And contracted diseases venereal:
The more vulgar-minded say "pox".

The dazzling peak of perfection,
*There wasn't a ***** she would scorn,*
She gave every man an erection:
*The more vulgar-minded say "****".*

Did you ever see Anna make water?
It's a sight that you ought not to miss.
She can lead for a mile and a quarter:
The more vulgar-minded say "piss".

*If I had two ***** like a bison*
*And a ***** like a big buffalo,*
I would sit on the edge of creation
And piss on the buggers below.

Once a boy was no good,
    took a girl into a wood,
Bye, bye, Blackbird.
Laid her down upon the grass,
Pinched her **** and slapped her ****,
Bye, bye, Blackbird.
Took her where nobody else could find her,
To a place where he could really grind her,
Rolled her over on her front,
Shoved his ***** right up her ****.
Blackbird, bye, bye.

But this girl was no sport,
Took her story to a court,
Bye, bye, Blackbird.
Told her story in the morn,
All the jury had a ****,
Blackbird, bye, bye.
Then the judge came to his decision,
This poor sod got eighteen months in prison,
So next time, boy, do it right,
Stuff her **** with dynamite
Blackbird bye, bye.

CHARLOTTE THE HARLOT LAY DYING

Charlotte the Harlot lay dying,
A piss-pot supported her head,
The blow-flies were buzzing around her,
She lay on her left *** and said:

Chorus: "I've been had
        by the army, the navy,
        By a bullfighting toreador,
        By dagos and drongos and dingos,
        But never by maggots before.
        So roll back
        your dirty old ****holes
        And give me the cream
        of your ****."
        So they rolled back
        their dirty old ****holes,
        And played "Home Sweet Home"
        on her guts.

Charlotte the Harlot repented,
She'd never have another bang,
She wanted to go to heaven,
So she rolled on her right tit and sang:

Charlotte·the Harlot was buried
The town was much quieter than before,
But one night at the local brothel
Her ghost it appeared in the door:

CHRISTOPHER COLUMBO

In fourteen hundred and ninety-two
A man whose name was Chris
Stood by the Trevi fountain
Indulging in a piss.

*Chorus: His ***** they were so round—o*
*His **** hung to the ground—o*
That fornicating, copulating
Son-of-a-bitch Columbo.

Along did come the Queen of Spain
And glimpsing there his dong,
Forthwith was smitten with desire
And knew not right from wrong.

"Oh, Isabelle," Columbo said,
*A-waving of his *****,*
"The world is round as these are,
I feel that duty calls."

"Just wait a bit," said Isabelle,
"And don't forget essentials,
For I've a mind to have a grind
And check on your credentials."

She gave her guest no time for rest,
The pace was fairly killing,
With legs apart he gave the tart
A cream and cherry filling.

For forty days and forty nights
He sailed the broad Atlantic,
Columbo and his scurvy crew
For want of a screw were frantic.

And when they got to Yankee land
They spied a Yankee harlot
When they came her **** was lily-white
When they left her **** was scarlet.

With lustful shout they ran about
And practised copulation,
And when they left to sail away
They'd doubled the population.

And when his men pulled out again,
And reckoned all their score up,
They'd caught a pox from every box
That syphilized all Europe.

The Completely Draining Experience

UP THE CISTERN

A lavish celebration of the smallest room

JAMES RIDDLE

A wind in the ear of all you big spenders, who pass on average at least six days a year closeted away – you can all come out now; you'll never need to feel non-loo again! Relief at last, in this penetrating exploration of the Great British Obsession. Relax (and discover):

* WHAT happens if you cover the loo-pan with cling film and wait for the unsuspecting user to create a stink
* WHO said 'The evil that men do lives after them'
* IF you're ready to blast off for the executive toilet, or always bogged down on the outside, waiting for life's 'ENGAGED' sign to become 'VACANT'

PLUS

piles of other banal retentions, loophemisms and moving verses

IN

The only book guaranteed to put bums back on seats – and fill every loo in the land!

COMPLETELY EXPURGATED VERSION

NON-FICTION/HUMOUR   0 7221 7350 4   £1.75

BACHELOR BOYS

THE YOUNG ONES'

BOOK

BEN ELTON · LISE MAYER · RIK MAYALL

Call it bad karma or anarchy in the U.K., there's never been anything quite like the cult-hit T.V. series *The Young Ones* — totally bizarre, totally original, totally aggressive and . . . totally TOTAL. So, here are the Young Ones in their own write at last: Rick the Radical Poet, Vyvyan the Psychopathic Punk, Neil the Suicidal Hippy, and Mike, the Would-Be Spiv. Together they reveal The Ultimate Truth About Everything to their avid fans, including absolutely zillions of helpless hints on:

★ HOBBIES
Neil's 101 really interesting things to do with a tea-cup
★ FILTH
Some kissing hints from Vyvyan. Lesson one: Snog the Dog
★ LAUGHS
Including Rick's only joke: These are my pants and I'm sticking to them!!!
PLUS
a controversial statement from the Acne Liberation Front. The Young Ones say: WEAR YOUR SPOTS WITH PRIDE

NON-FICTION/HUMOUR   0 7221 5765 7   £2.9

*EVERYTHING YOU NEED TO KNOW ABOUT SPORT
(AND A LOT OF THINGS YOU DON'T)!*

The Book Of
SPORTS
LISTS

CRAIG AND DAVID BROWN

Who 'floats like a butterfly and stings like one too'?
Who gave up sex for a year in order to improve his game
– and what does it cost to persuade John McEnroe to
play with your racquets for a year? Which sportsman
said 'I'd give my right arm to be a pianist' – and what do
Torvill and Dean have to say about each other?

THE BOOK OF SPORTS LISTS brings together the
most remarkable things ever done and the funniest
things ever said in the name of sport around the world.
Record-breakers and blunderers, prudes and Casanovas,
good sports and bad sports, they're all in THE BOOK OF
SPORTS LISTS.

NON-FICTION/HUMOUR/SPORT   0 7221 1935 6   £2.50

*Don't miss Craig Brown and Lesley Cunliffe's THE
BOOK OF ROYAL LISTS, also available in Sphere
Books.*

STRANGE THINGS

ROBERT K. G. TEMPLE

DID YOU KNOW THAT . . .

There may be two suns in the solar system!

Canaries lose a fifth of their brains in the winter – but get it all back in the spring!

The lesbian whiptail lizards of America clone their offspring!

There are planets in our galaxy which are 17% crystallized diamonds!

Some birds have a fear of flying!

STRANGE THINGS:

a bizarre, baffling and mind-boggling guide to the quirks of nature, including . . . heavy-breathing water lilies, sun-tanned eggs, irate embryos, perfumed moths, sensitive sponges, mathematical monkeys, over-sexed fruitflies and many other wonders.

SCIENCE   0 7221 8410 7   £1.50

A SELECTION OF BESTSELLERS FROM SPHERE

FICTION

SMART WOMEN	Judy Blume	£2.25 ☐
INHERITORS OF THE STORM	Victor Sondheim	£2.95 ☐
HEADLINES	Bernard Weinraub	£2.75 ☐
TRINITY'S CHILD	William Prochnau	£2.50 ☐
THE SINISTER TWILIGHT	J. S. Forrester	£1.95 ☐

FILM & TV TIE-INS

WATER	Gordon McGill	£1.75 ☐
THE RADISH DAY JUBILEE	Sheilah B. Bruce	£1.50 ☐
THE RIVER	Steven Bauer	£1.95 ☐
THE DUNE STORYBOOK	Joan D. Vinge	£2.50 ☐
ONCE UPON A TIME IN AMERICA	Lee Hays	£1.75 ☐

NON-FICTION

THE *WOMAN* BOOK OF LOVE AND SEX	Deidre Sanders	£1.95 ☐
PRINCESS GRACE	Steven Englund	£2.50 ☐
MARGARET RUTHERFORD – A BLITHE SPIRIT	Dawn Langley Simmons	£1.95 ☐
BARRY FANTONI'S CHINESE HOROSCOPES	Barry Fantoni	£1.75 ☐
THE STEP-PARENT'S HANDBOOK	Elizabeth Hodder	£2.95 ☐

All Sphere books are available at your local bookshop or newsagent, or can be ordered direct from the publisher. Just tick the titles you want and fill in the form below.

Name_____

Address_____

_____

Write to Sphere Books, Cash Sales Department, P.O. Box 11, Falmouth, Cornwall TR10 9EN

Please enclose cheque or postal order to the value of the cover price plus:

UK: 55p for the first book, 22p for the second book and 14p per copy for each additional book ordered to a maximum charge of £1.75.

OVERSEAS: £1.00 for the first book and 25p per copy for each additional book.

BFPO & EIRE: 55p for the first book, 22p for the second book plus 14p per copy for the next 7 books, thereafter 8p per book.

Sphere Books reserve the right to show new retail prices on covers which may differ from those previously advertised in the text or elsewhere, and to increase postal rates in accordance with the PO.